legacy AFTER loss

BOOKS BY CHELSEA OHLEMILLER

Now That She's Gone

Legacy After Loss

legacy AFTER loss

THE SACRED WORK OF REMEMBERING, REBUILDING, AND ENDURING THROUGH GRIEF

CHELSEA OHLEMILLER

Revell
a division of Baker Publishing Group
Grand Rapids, Michigan

Published by Revell
a division of Baker Publishing Group
Grand Rapids, Michigan
RevellBooks.com

Printed in the United States of America

Library of Congress Cataloging-in-Publication Data
Names: Ohlemiller, Chelsea, 1982– author
Title: Legacy after loss : the sacred work of remembering, rebuilding, and enduring through grief / Chelsea Ohlemiller.
Description: Grand Rapids, Michigan : Revell, a division of Baker Publishing Group, [2026] |
Identifiers: LCCN 2026009712 | ISBN 9780800748159 paperback | ISBN 9781493455614 ebook
Subjects: LCSH: Loss (Psychology) | Grief | Bereavement—Psychological aspects
Classification: LCC BF575.G7 O295 2026
LC record available at https://lccn.loc.gov/2026009712

Cover illustration by Leah Von Fange

Published in association with Books & Such Literary Management, www.booksandsuch.com.

Baker Publishing Group publications use paper produced from sustainable forestry practices and postconsumer waste whenever possible.

26 27 28 29 30 31 32 7 6 5 4 3 2 1

Hattie, Hutson & Hyland—

You are the best part of my story, the best part of my life.
My greatest accomplishments will forever be the three of you.
Love you to the moon and back and back—always.

xox

Justin—

Thank you for being the kind of man who takes
my breath away and also reminds me to breathe.

xox

contents

HOPE

HEALING FOREVER

MEMORIES

LESSONS & STRENGTH

THEIR LEGACY

LIVING AGAIN

FAITH

MY LEGACY (& YOURS TOO)

introduction

My first book, *Now That She's Gone: A Daughter's Reflections on Loss, Love, and a Mother's Legacy*, was a space of raw grief and fresh loss. It was a depiction of the messiness of grief and the transformations that take place afterward. This book is for the *after*—after the final goodbye and beyond the fresh grief. It's for after you've found your breath again and after the shock and daze of death's consequences and responsibilities. For some it may be shortly after, for others it might be quite a long time after—either way, this book is for you when you're ready to step beyond the pain and into what remains, both the beautiful and the unexpected.

My journey to the after wasn't quick, and it wasn't easy. It took me a while to get here, to this place that holds more hope than pain and more worthwhile reminiscence than repeating the moments of my mother's passing in my head like a vicious cycle of heartbreak. But I'm here and I'm grateful for the path of healing that has led me to this place—the *now*, a collaboration of many things, the most impactful of them all, perspective.

I decided to let grief be my motivator instead of letting it be my excuse to pause my life and also my mother's legacy and her continued influence. I made a choice to use the new perspective that healing has provided and place my pain below my pursuit to courageously live, not just survive. I'm learning how to eagerly step forward in her honor and her memory instead of staying weighed down by a blanket of grief that consumes both her legacy and my own.

I'm in a constant pursuit of healing and of continued gratitude for both a life still left to live and a life that I was so blessed to be a part of—hers. My hope is that you are too, no matter who you've lost or when.

This book is my vulnerable navigation from lost and numb to found and awakened. It's the transition from hopelessness to rediscovering that hope is an achievable feat, when you're ready and open to it. It's the blending of holding both an absence and a presence, neither of which are accurate in the ways you were taught before grief and loss. It's my all-in commitment to ensure my mother's life, instead of her death, defines my days—an achievement I think all our lost loved ones would choose for us.

Are you ready to step into life again? Are you ready to step into healing and hope? Are you ready to step into the making of legacies, both yours and theirs?

Step into the after, friends. I'm stepping with you.

xox, Chels

Disclaimer: This book is filled with reflections and free-flowing thoughts from the diverse spaces of my grief journey. They do not, and are not designed to, reflect true biblical content or theology, but are instead the vulnerable and creative expressions of someone experiencing profound loss. I am not an expert. I am simply someone living with grief. Please read with grace and understanding.

after goodbye

"We all have different reasons for forgetting to breathe—
mine is the death of my mother."

XOX, Chels

somewhere beautiful

Time is slipping from us, from you, faster than the sand in one of those fancy hourglasses. You've lost your ability to communicate. Hopefully you haven't lost your ability to listen. You always said you weren't afraid for what's coming, even though I always have been. You tried to prepare me for this moment, but none of the planning has lessened the ache and devastation of what is happening.

I vow to be unselfish in this unimaginable moment. All you've given must now be returned, even when it feels impossible. You always acted with faith and love and light and, more than anything, hope that when your time comes and death finds you, it is only an ending for us, as you are headed somewhere beautiful.

Though I find myself jealous of this glorious place and of the others who have found eternity there, I know it is a place you're worthy of—a destination you've aspired toward your entire life. I know you're headed somewhere beautiful, and yet here I am, praying you'd be able to stay here in this imperfect and often burdensome world, with me, with us. But staying would mean being attached to a disease and its pain for longer. It would add quantity to your days, but it wouldn't have the power to include quality of life with them.

To ease my worry, to lessen my fear, I meditate on the hope that you're headed somewhere beautiful.

You're headed to a place where pain cannot find you and diseases have been eradicated. A place filled with only beauty, joy, and peace. You're headed to a place where eternal life is the gift and your view holds constant light, not by the sun or the moon, but by the only other person, besides your family, you've lived your life for—God.

In so many selfish ways, I've often prayed for you to stay, to remain here, to be here with me longer, if only for mere days or another brief moment. But now, sitting in the truth of your experience, and the depth of all that you're enduring, I can't wait for you to head someplace beautiful.

Even with a heart that will nearly shatter and a soul that will ache for you each day, I pray you reach somewhere beautiful, somewhere called heaven.

You deserve heaven's peace and pureness; you've worked toward them with a firm and steady faith. I can't wait for you to be healed with a simple touch and for you to be graced with the ultimate form of perfection—his.

My entire life I've been mesmerized by your beauty. I cannot begin to conceptualize how beautiful you'll be when your health has been restored and you experience the fulfillment of all of God's promises.

Soon, everything will change—for the both of us. The day you drift to that beautiful place, I will begin my journey with grief while it will solidify your journey with God. The hope is that one is temporary, the other permanent.

Find heaven. Find peace. Find your way to someplace beautiful, and when you do, save a space for me.

The goal has always been to find and forever stay somewhere beautiful.

after goodbye

What comes after goodbye, the final goodbye, when sacred bodies have been laid to rest and placed six feet below—unreachable? When headstones decorate the memorable spaces where loved ones' bodies will forever be? What happens after the responsibilities of death and decisions?

What happens in the after, not theirs but ours?

The one where the days are still coming and the world is still spinning, but you feel stuck—nauseated by the movement and immobilized by the pain. The days when the sun still rises and sets, but you don't see either because you're locked in an invisible confinement, one you never knew existed until now—one called "grief."

What happens in the after, not theirs but ours—the after "they're gone," the after "they're in a better place," the after "them," and even worse, the after "us" when we were together? What happens when they pass on to greatness and glory and you remain—heartbroken by their absence and confused by life's workings and, dare I say, sometimes even God's decisions?

What comes to fill the holes that were created by loss or to mend the slices that have been carved into what feels like every piece of your body and, even more harshly, your soul? What comes to take the pain, or at least hide it? What comes to shield your newfound fears and your consistent and always present, always dominating anxieties?

What comes to save us in the after? What comes to fill the void?

The answer is you.

One day you realize that the only way to heal, the only way to survive, the only way to keep stepping into new days is to walk them yourself. You realize that you can do hard things in the service of something that matters. And for you, what matters are the people who are still here—your children, your family, your friends—the ones who remain. For them, you can and will do anything. Which means you must not simply survive—you must heal. You must live again. You must step forward even when the future is now unknown and unrecognizable to the one that you had built in your heart and mind.

The answer is you.

You are the only one with the power and the capability to untie yourself from all of the bindings that are holding you back and holding you down. You are the only one who gets to decide how you will live from now on with both the grief and the life still left to live. Eventually, you'll find that both are vital for success and transformation in the days to come.

You are the creator of the after. You are the architect, and you are the author, so build and write delightfully. But more importantly, make sure you're building and writing. Don't let the pause and immobility that come with heartbreak and loss steal the momentum of your days.

The after, your after, is what you make of it. So, when you're ready, breathe and heal, and then make something they'd be proud of.

dear you, after the funeral

A Letter to You, the One Who Has Just Left the Funeral

The funeral is over. It feels like your future is too. The sun feels sharp and blinding. The air feels thick and unnatural. You find yourself drifting to each next thing, never fully comprehending how you got there.

You buried someone you love and also so many pieces of what you thought would be—pieces of who you thought you'd be. You can't imagine what will become of you.

Me. You become me.

The woman of now, the woman who has had years separating her from that day, the one who is seared into both her mind and heart, the one who finalized it all.

You become me.

It doesn't happen quickly, and it's certainly not without its challenges, but with time and care, you become me, and I become the next version of you.

In simple terms, that means you survive this. Your life continues.

The in-between from your now and mine will not be friendly, and it will not be kind. Heartbreak and sorrow fill the atmosphere that surrounds you in ways that cannot be undone or ignored. Healing will be on your to-do list every single day. Most days you'll ignore the list completely. Even now we work toward healing, though we're much better listeners today—thankfully.

I'll skip the rest of the intricacies and destruction from the in-between. Not because it isn't important or foundational to both our life and our grief, but because it finds you, finds us, no matter how hard we try to evade it.

Neither you, nor I, could ever stop the consequences and the aftermath of grief.

Grief happens. Mourning happens. Pain happens. We never find a way to outrun it, eventually we learn we didn't need to.

Through all of it, we're here—in the now.

My now is what I wish you could see, or at the very least feel the hope that it exists. I wish I could travel to you. I'd wrap you in hope and light. I'd very delicately and simply tell you that all of this is survivable, that you will survive. After all, the existence of me is proof.

I'd tell you that you will stay—even when you thought you didn't want to and even through the times you felt like staying was an impossible task. I'd tell you nothing but truth, though I know if we were face-to-face, you'd believe it all to be lies. It would not be lies.

You will fall, but I, the future version of you, assure you—you will rise. You do the work and the healing and all of that eventually leads to me—to us.

Right now, walking away from this funeral, this newly buried body, this fresh loss, you have no concept of anything other than loss and pain and anger and disbelief, but one day you will. You'll look back at the woman walking away from the closed casket of this funeral, and she'll be unrecognizable to you. And yet, even still, you'll hold a deep knowing that you should be proud of her—which, of course, is really you.

She hurt deeply but she healed and is healing still. She let reminiscence create more, be more, than regret or relentless ache and agony. She decided to be something—both a life and a legacy.

She is you. She is me. She is us.
We make it.

We make it because of you—that wounded woman who walked away from that funeral shattered, forever changed, and eventually determined. Determined to give me a chance, to give a future you a chance.

And you did.
And we make it.

You're going to make it. I'm proof.
From both of us, both the torn and the transformed—thank you.

be with us

A whisper to heaven, to them—

Be with us, in whatever way you can, in whatever way God allows from above. May we still be guided by your influence and your love. May we still find spaces meant for us and steer away from things that aren't part of our unique design, as you taught us in the past.

Please, be with us.

When it feels like we're abandoning you with each new year that rolls in, stay in the memories and the reminiscence. May you stay in our hearts and in our minds. Never leave.

Please, stay with us.

When we feel like you're slipping further away and in times where the empty space, the one that you used to occupy, feels like it will suffocate us, may we remember that death did not change the love or the relationship. You have never been fully gone, for pieces of you remain in us—always. Your love and your light were too powerful to diminish or fade.

Please, remind us.

When you look from heaven and see us celebrating, engaged in joyous displays of happy moments, but also with an ache in our soul for a moment that you're missing, please be with us. Send us signs of your love and your memory. Send us reminders of your presence. Send us tangible things that make it undeniable that you're still here, in your own way, from heaven.

Please be with us.

As we enter into new chapters that feel like they don't contain you, may we remember that they do. As we start to tell others that yet another year is added to the tally of how long you've been gone, fill our hearts with your influence and your faith and your hope. The ultimate truth is that it marks only how many years since your death and that you've never truly been gone—you remain, in beautiful and invisible and unexpected ways. You remain in coincidence and in memory. You remain in ways too bold and brilliant for us to attempt to comprehend.

You remain, and that is a glorious truth that carries us.

Please, be with us—not just now, but always.
However you can, be with us.

this home was once ours

Both the garage door and front door have been painted teal. It looks just as wrong as it feels. Even worse, suddenly I despise people I've never met. Not only have they changed things with paint, they've managed to cut down the tree my grandfather planted and also the one my mother intentionally selected when building and dreaming up this home.

Lucky for both the new owners, and me, they've managed to keep my mother's flower beds looking beautiful, though different than she always kept them. I think if they had been decimated too, I'd find myself knocking on the door and asking why they're trying to erase the hard work of the woman and family that used to live here—proof that memories were made before them.

It might not sting as much if this house didn't feel like more than just wood and windows. It might not hurt as intensely if my mother's next home wasn't a combination of a casket covered in six feet of dirt and heaven. Because of these truths, the changes made to this house feel brutal and compassionless.

I wonder what changes have been made inside. The answer is probably much too harsh for my heart and my mind.

I wonder which things they kept the same, untouched by their desire to mark their new territory. Which things did they feel were worthy of staying just as they are? Were there any? I'll never know, but also, I'm not sure I want to. I'm already provoked by the transformations on the outside and the artistic choices they've made to cover my mother's.

If they saw me staring at their house, the way I'm currently doing safely from the driver's side of my vehicle, would they recognize the way I once belonged here—the way this place was once mine in such an intimate way it would stay with me forever? Would they understand the sentimental tethers this home has on my heart and that the only reason we sold it is because we had to? My mother left us rich in love and influence, but not rich enough to keep her house and also our own.

First, we said goodbye to our mother, then we said goodbye to the things of hers we could not keep—either financially impossible or physically impossible, limited by space and capacity. Losing our mother was the most difficult of our losses, but losing this house, the space that held her greatness and her life's moments, that generated deep grief too.

I grew up hearing "There's no place like home," in a house where a wooden sign that read "Home is where the heart is" hung. And now I stare at that same place as a stranger, an outsider. I'm staring at a place that seems both familiar and unrecognizable. How can that be?

As I slowly shift the car into drive, I realize, I don't despise these homeowners, though at that first teal glance it felt like it. I despise the truths and happenings that made this house theirs, giving them the opportunity to do just that—make it theirs. I despise that in death many things get renovated and replaced, not out of choice but out of necessity. My mother left this house for her grave, death's consequence. I detached from this house, also death's consequence. Who knew death caused casualties beyond the breath and heartbeats stolen from someone you love?

This house is now a representation of the multiple losses rippled into existence from the death of someone cherished and adored. This home has changed just as harshly and as palpably as I have. Grief does that, I've learned.

Maybe the teal doors sting because they showcase unwanted and unchosen change—both for this house and for me. Teal paint hides the previous beige shade and the story of what once was. Only those of us who called this house home will remember the memories and people held inside this space.

Maybe that's what I'm authentically and vulnerably afraid of, that this is just another involuntary change, knowing that with change comes the opportunity to forget—not just her but also all of us.

I don't want her influence to be erased or her life to be forgotten. I don't want any of us to be forgotten—not just from the world, but from the spaces where we once existed so beautifully. May this house serve not as a place where we've been erased but rather as a space where memories and influence live on beyond changed paint colors and redesigned garden beds and living rooms.

This home was once ours. Now it belongs to someone new. The memories, however, they're ours indefinitely—imprinted in ways that cannot be changed or erased.

The new owners can change the paint colors as many times as they want, we'll always know what lies beneath and the colors secretly hidden underneath the surface. And I realize, what a beautiful secret it is to hold—our own knowing, our own memory, our own remembrance.

funeral home

I walk into the funeral home, and the smell immediately has my head in a cinematic replay of every person I've known who has lain in a casket in a place just like this one.

As I stand, rooted in grief, in the front entrance of this profound space, I wonder if there is a casket filled with someone right now. The parking lot was empty, but that doesn't mean there are no lifeless bodies here, tucked out of sight until just the right moment. Will this room be filled later today with the hearts and souls of individuals who are hurting?

The entryway is full of beautiful flowers, probably fake, a way to extend their longevity, something life cannot offer, time slipping away so quickly from each one of us. I can feel both the sacredness that these walls must hold and also the harshness. This building encapsulates the tangled emotions of both life and death.

Tears fill my eyes, and I wonder how many tears have been released here. I wonder if those tears had been collected, would they mirror a lake or something larger, like an ocean? I wonder how many people have come here to mourn and then return later to be mourned, experiencing each extreme this space can offer.

When this building was designed and constructed, was it handled with care knowing what would take place here? Did the crew know what the foundation would hold or what the walls would witness? Was it blessed by faith or the church to conduct the business of goodbyes? Is there a certification or license you must hold to serve grief like bars serve liquor? There should be.

Surrounded by death and clients who lack breath and heartbeats, do funeral directors feel overwhelming gratitude for the thousands of breaths and beats their own bodies still produce? Does having death as a coworker change you—and if so, is it for better or for worse? Can it be both?

Pulling into the parking lot of this funeral home today made my stomach feel a bit homesick, but standing inside, smelling the distinct scent that can only be associated with death and longing, I'm being chiseled by grief again. It's as if I'm once again entering these doors to close the casket on those I've lost, the harshest being my mother.

Places like this one, with walls and windows that encapsulate final goodbyes, feel both so sacred and so bleak. They remind us of those we've lost and the fickle and unrelenting nature of grief and mourning.

I realize this funeral home, and all the others like it, is the kind of place that holds suffering and also memories of suffering. It's the kind of place that has you in present pain each time you step inside but also reliving pain from all the previous goodbyes too. This place also holds other things like honor and reminiscence, but grief and suffering are the largest and most intense, the most potent.

Most people don't like these spaces, and I can see why. They are like personal portals leading back to the harshest pain you've ever experienced and enduring it all over again simply by walking inside.

My grief won't dissipate until I can get back out into the fresh air and feel both the warmth and the hope of the sun. For now, I must sit with these feelings and these reflections of loss, death, and grief—life's unavoidable realities.

This place is constructed by both love and sadness. And so am I since losing someone I love. Does that make me a walking funeral home, housing both life and death always—my life, their death?

Maybe that is grief's challenge, to be a space that holds it all—similar to this funeral home.

uninvited

The casket is closed and then eventually lowered beneath the soil, too far for me to reach, too far for me to touch just one more time so that I can feel the sacredness of this moment. Soon this hole will be filled with dirt, and even further into the tomorrows there will be a stone carved with the name of someone I'm now required to live without.

Can you be uninvited from your life and the future that you constructed so carefully in your mind and in all the diaries and doodles of your past? Can you be uninvited from plans that felt like they were solidified with intentionality and trust that life is fully livable and God is fully good?

Can you be uninvited from life, your life? Or are you simply uninvited from the togetherness of lives combined and experiences shared? Are we instead uninvited from the *we* and transported into the *I*?

Holding a loss I wasn't prepared for, I certainly feel dishearteningly uninvited—from life and hope and all the beauty of togetherness. I feel uninvited from faith and from strength. I feel uninvited from the naivety that miracles can happen, even in the after. I feel uninvited and instead like an intruder of my own life, and sometimes like a prisoner.

Either way, the tomorrows come and come and come, along with the grief and the mourning. The aftermath of loss led to a grave filled with dirt, then decorated with a headstone, both beautiful and harsh. Oh, the irony—our loved ones are tucked into a blessed box, lowered into the ground, while all of the empty spaces around them are filled, pressed down, compounded, until there is not a tiny speck of emptiness that remains. All the while, my holes, my brokenness, my sharp internal edges, are raw and open and uninhabited. My newly vacant spaces cannot be filled, they remain as poignant reminders of the stolen *we*, and *us*, and *unity*—all built by love.

Now, I sit in this place, this graveyard, again and again, with one-sided conversations, a visible grief, and a heartbreak that seems to radiate more vulnerable and brighter each time I enter.

Here, I am always invited—into the pain and into the longing, and on good days the reminiscence too. Here I am always welcome. Cemeteries don't turn people away, neither the living nor the deceased. They are a place of constant invitation, either to rest or to visit, and sometimes both.

Ironic that it was in this place I became uninvited, untethered from my life before loss. It was this place that revealed life's finite ways and the permanent places that become a body's final destination. It was also here that I was welcomed into the *after*, into the life that was chosen and designed for me, not the one I envisioned and built myself. A design some would suggest is more worthy than my own. Me, I'm still dreaming of an invitation back into the *before*, where they were here, and we were together, and all felt right and just.

But you cannot return to the before. It exists as only a memory. I still have the chance to be more than a memory—even in this edited and revised version of the life I planned and wanted.

Turns out, you can't be uninvited from your life, only detached from the pieces of it that were created by you. You can only be separated from the visions that you planned for, not the truths of what life is or will be.

Life itself is an invitation—to live until you can't and to love just the same.

What will *we* invite into our lives? This is the bigger question. The one with the ability to impact what comes, the one with actionable choice of things that matter. Things like hope, resiliency, healing, and the bold intention to find purpose and appreciation for what remains—because there are priceless things that remain.

Grief comes as an uninvited guest in our lives, yet it's one we must make room for. *How will you make room?* Tell me, how will you make room?

what's wrong with you

You cry. You weep. You wonder what is wrong with you. You know there is something wrong. In fact, it's probably too many things to list, too many things to comprehend. You wonder if numbers count that high.

People say this is grief. They say this is mourning. It feels like more than that. It feels like a helplessness and a hopelessness that covers and consumes you and life in general. It's as if you've forgotten how to breathe and then suddenly remember you must, so your breath is labored and unnatural, similar to your heartbeat.

Someone you love died, but your health seems to have been depleted too. You wonder if this is what dying feels like, if this is dying.

You wonder what is wrong with you because there is something wrong with you. Not just the emptiness you both feel and see but the physical and emotional components too. You can't describe what is happening or how it feels in a way that's accurate, but you want to.

You think of calling an ambulance. You consider going to the ER. You know they'll diagnose it as anxiety while you silently scream and plead for answers that are scientifically sound. You've lived with anxiety all of your life. It isn't this, is it? You should call a therapist, and you will, eventually. Maybe they'll help you find out what is wrong and even better, maybe they'll fix it. Maybe they'll fix you.

You definitely need fixing.
You need healing.
You need recovery from this pain and this circumstance.

Can you heal from the wounds of death? Can you heal from the wounds of a forever absence? How do you recover from wounds so raw and deep that you won't allow them to be seen or known, and certainly not touched?

You wonder what on earth is wrong with you. You wonder if people will accept you as you are—different. You wonder how you'll ever be loved again. Will you be loved again in a way that's pure and effortless and real, like someone once showed you, not in a romantic way but one that was personal?

You wonder what is wrong with you.

You cry and weep and scream, "What is wrong with me?"

And you hear, even if only in your heart—

I love everything that is wrong with you, because it's not wrong at all. It's so real and vulnerable and true that it cannot be ignored, nor would I want it to be. Your tears and your breathlessness are proof that you love without hesitation and without any limitations.

The only thing wrong with you is the fact that you're now void of someone irreplaceable, someone special. The only thing wrong with you is the empty space that follows you in every place you go and the headstone that has replaced the home and person you always visited. Those are the wrongs. The things that shouldn't be.

There is nothing wrong with you. Do not attach yourself to the grief or the pain. They are part of you, but they are not you. You are beautiful and you are hurting and you are void of someone you love, but I promise, there is nothing wrong with you.

Each piece of this is true, whether the voice of God or the whispers of hope. And while you don't believe it now, you know one day you will. You can understand that you are not what's wrong, but rather the myths and misconceptions of what you should be feeling and how you should be healing are. Some of this pain and heaviness comes from the world's view of how you should hold the reality of loss, how you should carry the responsibility.

The wrong isn't you.

The wrong is the fact that they're no longer here. The wrong is the world thinking that there is a right way to grieve or that grief has a timeline. The wrong is thinking that time heals all wounds and that closure is something achievable. The wrong is believing that busyness lets you escape pain or that faith can somehow erase it.

The wrong isn't grief itself but everything we've been taught about it.

We sit and mourn and think that something is wrong with us when the reality is that something is wrong with the expectations of loss, not the experience of loss itself and the way we make it individual and unique.

The wrong isn't you.

On your harshest days, in your deepest grief, remember, the wrong isn't you and it never will be.

I promise, the wrong isn't you.

marked by grief

You step into the shower. You hope you can wash grief off like you do the dirt that sometimes finds you. Instead, it's more like sand. Pieces of it will stay with you long after this shower. You'll find it in your clothes, in your bags, and still glued to spaces of your body that you've intentionally and diligently scrubbed.

You cannot wash grief away. Like sand, grief finds spaces that you cannot reach and crevices you didn't even know exist.

You cannot scrub off heartbreak or pain. Once it arrives it is etched onto you like a tattoo, like a personal inscription, proof of the people and things you've lost. It stays to remind you that you are forever marked by this event, this death.

But markings aren't always cruel, and they certainly aren't always harsh. Markings can also be priceless and breathtaking in ways that say, *I was loved. I was cared for. I mattered.*

Markings can be proof of things that no longer exist and times that have shifted to memory. They can serve as artwork for remembering and also for asking—so that when others see your stamps from grief, they'll want to learn about times they weren't privy to and people they never met. They'll want to know stories and names. You'll want to share stories and names.

Grief's brandings will become your conversation starter, your personal icebreaker. And this is why they stay, permanent and noticeable, just like the influence and the memory of those you've lost. Grief's scars, grief's markings, are meant to serve as reminders of the way death can change lives and how love does the same. They begin from pain and from deep sorrow, but they heal from grit and remembrance and resiliency.

Because you have grit and remembrance and resiliency.

You don't need to wash the grief away. You don't need to cover or hide grief's imprint. You need to surrender to the transformation. Knowing that, yes, the cost of this transformation was someone you loved, but they also get to be a creator of it too. Their lives weren't for nil; their advice wasn't for nothing. It was just as much for the *then* as it is for the *now*. For this. For you. For when they're gone.

Don't wash away your grief. Don't try to hide its markings. Embrace that you are imprinted with names and stories and memories that changed you. Let them change you and let that change be positive.

The grief from pain and loss brands you but also reminds you and permanently marks you with the truth: **You are loved. You are cared for. And you matter—still, always, forever.**

don't let me go

The hospital bed looks different in a house, a home. It doesn't belong here. They don't belong here—the one to die and the others to watch it all. Only one of them has accepted what will happen here, it's her—the one labeled terminal, the one placed in hospice. The others are still demanding miracles and in hopeless denial of what is to come.

She seems to know that her breaths are numbered, as are her heartbeats. She says, "I love you. I wish I could say it a million more times, but time is unfortunately more finite than we expected. Things are already in motion to stop, to end. My love is not one of them. It cannot and will not ever cease to exist—remember that, especially on days when loneliness and grief feel like a pit you cannot climb out of. Hold my memory with joy. Hold my influence with grace. Hold my love with hope. Hold my legacy with all the beauty that remains. And please, from your hearts and your lives and your souls and your memory, don't let me go."

And the woman who will survive this day, this experience, the one who listened intently to every spoken word as if it were her mother's final prayer, she is speechless. And she knows she would never, could never, let her mother go. This woman will be the invisible beauty and strength inside her, always. She could never, would never, let her go.

Seated on the edge of the bed, she's sobbing, her husband holding her tight. The eulogy was read. The funeral concluded. The casket they so bravely chose has been lowered into the ground. There isn't another task, another responsibility, there is only the undeniable visibility of emptiness and the piercing ache of grief.

She cannot change the circumstances of life and death. She cannot rewind and go back. She is stuck, here, in this place of harshness, in this despised void that will now attach itself to every part of who she is and who she will be. When the realization of this truth hits her, she knows she needs her husband's strength as much as she needs her own. Her strength seems to have vanished as she desperately pleads, "Help me find the courage to step into tomorrow. Help me find hope. Help me find the pieces of me that have scattered and shattered so catastrophically they won't be recognizable if they can even be found. Right now, please don't let me go."

And he doesn't. He stays. He holds her. He doesn't let her go.

Settled into the freshly cut grass, seated crisscross and perfectly aligned with the etched name of someone she's lost, she mourns. This place is designated for memorialization. For her, this place is designed for conversations that transcend to eternity. It's the place she searches for hope, light, and influence. She calls out, which sounds more like a prayer, though she's not speaking to God. She's speaking to the life that left too soon.

She looks up to the sky and she sorrowfully begs, "You've traveled further than I can see and further than I can comprehend. Please don't leave me fully. Tuck pieces of your influence and your love into each thing that I do and each version of myself that I become. Please don't let your death end our relationship. Instead let it extend beyond the moon and back like you used to say about your love when I was a child. Please, from here to wherever you are, don't let me go."

The consistent and common thread of life and endings and pain is a battle cry, a prayer, a pleading of "Don't let me go."

And they never have, and we never will—a shared promise of never letting go.

Always held. Always loved. Always in a delicate, yet unwavering form of togetherness—no boundaries, no limits.

We have each other, always—forever held.

And one day when we're reunited, together in eternity, I imagine we'll embrace and gently say again, "Please, don't let me go."

empty space

"If we moved backward instead,
I'd have you—always."

XOX, Chels

longing for heaven

She tells me that she used to be afraid of death and heaven and now she longs for it. She sometimes even yearns for it more intensely than she does her next breath. She said she aches for the place where her loved ones have ventured, some untimely, all before she was ready or accepting of a final goodbye.

She tells me that she longs to be whole again. She longs to be the version of herself that isn't chiseled by loss and torn apart by grief and heartbreak. She longs to be the version of herself that is healed of pain—the one that isn't missing pieces or scarred by life's messiness.

She wants to be herself again—the one who still has everyone she loves. Notice she said loves, not loved, because her love isn't past tense, even though most pieces of her life are. The past holds her mother, her grandmothers, her grandfathers, some friends, and many others, while her future doesn't. Each added day is void of so much—so many people.

She tells me life still holds beauty, but things are so much more complicated than before she lost people—before she lost them for good, which isn't really good at all, but forever. She tells me that once you watch a life end and witness the impact of "rest in peace," you are never the same.

She is never the same.

She tells me she'll never be—and maybe she wouldn't want to be, because grief has changed her. Love also changed her. And if she had to choose which one changed her most, she says it would be love. Sure, grief changed her in harsh and painful ways, but love changed her in glorious ways that cannot be dimmed or lessened because of hard times or harsh moments.

So yes, she longs for heaven in ways she never has before. At first, the death of someone she loved had her wishing she could send herself too. But now, now that the weight of grief has lightened, now that she sees more reminiscence than emptiness—now she longs for heaven in different ways.

Now, she longs for heaven in ways that keep her grounded here on earth in light, in hope, and in the pursuit to make this place a little more heaven-esque, just like the legacy she was gifted revealed to her. That incredible person she lost, their hope was that she would carry on living for the both of them—longing for heaven, eventually but not currently.

So yes, she longs for heaven, and while she waits for her turn to be reunited with the person she misses so fiercely, she stays. She stays and lives for the both of them—the one in heaven and the one longing for it.

She longs for heaven—eventually, but for now she has legacies to create and living that she's still been blessed with. May we all be like her and long for heaven—not just in our pain but in our life too.

to have them back

You say you'd do anything, trade anything, to have them back, but you wouldn't. Not if it meant continued pain and illness. Not if it meant more withering away and a complete depletion of their quality of life. You wouldn't wish them back how they were, their last physical form.

You wouldn't take away their heavenly status for an earthly one. Not with all you know about God and Jesus and eternity. You wouldn't take away their infinite healing for a finite one.

I know your heart might try to tell your mind that you'd do anything to have them back, but you wouldn't. Not if it meant they would return but, in doing so, be even less of themselves, still overcome by a disease that steals some of the best pieces of them—still stealing pieces of them if you bargained them back.

You wouldn't trade their full healing for a temporary one. You may not see it now or feel it yet in your heart, but you'd choose forever for them.

Forever healed.
Forever at peace.
Forever joyous.
Forever loved.
Forever them in their most perfect form.
Forever.

Now, when you say you'd do anything for them—it's true. You do it every day when you live without them. When you boldly feel gratitude for their heavenly restoration over your profound and significant grief, though it takes effort and always takes time and takes perspective. When you trust their faith and the Lord they prayed to their whole life, whether in the pews of a Sunday service or in the sacred places at home where they found him—over your own fear and disappointment—you do what's best for them.

Your love is so unwavering and selfless that you'd choose the best for them—always. Even if that means a temporary separation on this side of things. Your heart is more pure and noble than you give it credit for. Grief tries to dominate your wishes and your asks, and sometimes even your prayers—don't let it.

We wouldn't do anything to have them back if it meant an unraveling of all the greatness they witnessed immediately upon entering heaven. We wouldn't trade God's chosen path for them for our own pain to be eliminated. We wouldn't take away their gains in eternity to create added losses here on earth. We'd choose life for them in its most limitless form, which is exactly where they've journeyed and exactly where they always prayed they'd end up.

We'd do anything for them—anything, which means living without them for the rest of our lives until we meet again. And we will meet again.

negotiating the impossible

I never knew the hopelessness of trying to negotiate the impossible until I watched as someone's life faded—dissolving right in front of me. On my mother's deathbed, I tried to negotiate her healing. I never knew how much you could work toward something that simply cannot be, but even still, I persisted. I tried to create terms with God that would allow her to stay, fully healed. I tried to negotiate a miracle. One did not come.

I found myself negotiating again at her funeral. As I stared at her lifeless body, I begged and pleaded for it to be a dream, for the ability to detach myself from this nightmare that I found myself in, a plot I didn't want to be in. I promised to be better, and to do better, if she could be alive again. I confessed my sins, and I vowed to do whatever it took to have her back. My pleas and promises didn't work. We buried her mere hours later.

In the years that followed her death my negotiations never ceased, even though I knew that the chance of having them met with success was less than zero, impossible. It didn't stop the bargaining or the compromises I sent out into the universe or to heaven.

I asked, over and over again, for time to jump backward and for there to be a cure for each deadly disease that had impacted those I love. I asked for more time with those who found that time had slipped through their fingers like sand instead of collecting it like seashells on a beach. I asked for more memories and more photos. I asked for the need to say goodbye to come later than it did and for death to be something we hadn't witnessed yet.

I asked for things to be different. I asked for the impossible.

I never knew the hopelessness of trying to negotiate the impractical desires of my heart until I was met with years of failure and years of a lack of change in my situation—the absence of someone irreplaceable. It did not matter if I prayed or pleaded or demanded or asked politely. My asks, which felt like needs as important as air or water, could not be met with a rational solution, one my heart and soul yearned for.

One day I stopped negotiating the impossible. Instead, I started pleading for hope and reminders of a presence that even death cannot destroy. I started praying for representations of her influence instead of bargaining for pieces of the past. I started wishing for her in new ways—ways that were not ludicrous and unobtainable but instead realistic.

I started negotiating for love and hope and her presence in ways that were not always tangible, but real. I started negotiating for things that not only could be but already were surrounding me, if only I had the courage to pay attention—the willingness to see the creativity and craft in the love and impact of someone in eternity, someone absent in body but not in influence.

I realized there is no need to negotiate for the impossible when you live with the love and the legacy of someone profound and significant. The realities of their memory are still alive and powerful; we simply must keep reminding ourselves of that truth. We cannot change the past. We cannot undo the losses we've experienced and endured. We do not have that capability or that power. But we can be intentional with our hopes and wishes. We must use them to heal from our grief and then use that healing to pave the purpose of all that is to come—with our loved ones as our inspiration rather than a muse to create futures that cannot exist.

I no longer bargain for the impossible—life is not meant to be created from fantasy. Now, I stand in the truth that *is*, and I've found beauty more profound and meaningful than any illusion could ever promise. I found the powerful purpose in living life with attainable hopes and dreams, especially the one where we're reunited with all of our loved ones in heaven.

The possible is infinite, which is why now I look forward to what *will be* rather than what *can never be*. The hope is found there, in the possible.

just in case

Since learning how a heart can break and yet still beat in normal rhythm, I now work diligently to keep mine shielded from any pain that can be prevented. Just in case I'm able, I keep pieces of it guarded, both from love and loss, to ensure that if my heart breaks again, it won't shatter completely. There will be secret hiding spots that haven't been touched by anything—neither beauty nor atrocity.

Before watching life slip away from someone I loved, my whole heart was open and unlocked. I loved freely, untamed and wild. I gave my endearment like I handed out candy during trick-or-treat, quick and without thought. I always assumed the best in people and the best in circumstances. That was back when my heart was still whole, unchiseled by death, untouched by grief, and still naive to incurable diseases that can decimate the bodies of the unforgettable.

Once I saw the irreparable damage a heart can endure and still survive, I made portions of mine off-limits. Just in case I could tame the harshness of future losses, I created spaces in my heart and soul for me and *only* me. I vowed to never let another name or soul tether their influence to every part of me so that when something bad happened to them too, pieces of me would be left unscathed—something that hadn't happened the first time I lost someone so profoundly, someone irreplaceable.

I make sure to leave intentional open spaces and hidden places. A place can't hurt if it has never been seen or touched. It can't be hollowed and emptied if it has never been filled. Just in case devastation tries to find me again, I've got a tucked-away shelter for some of me—some of my heart.

And as I'm wrapping invisible caution tape around those certain pieces of my heart and soul, I realize none of the people I lost ever let their heart harden by life's catastrophes, nor did they mark off spaces of their soul to shield it from impending sorrow. They lived and loved abundantly until the very second they no longer could. They left no space unmarked or uninfluenced, which is why their personal impact was so powerful—it was a blend of all those who came before mixed with their own intentional and special touch created from both bravery and vulnerability.

It takes courage to allow yourself to be deeply impacted by life and love and all of the harsh and unavoidable in-betweens. It takes intentional boldness to let your entire self live fully. It creates vulnerabilities. It creates soft spaces. It creates foundational entities that can be eliminated at any time, without warning, and certainly without preparation.

But it also creates a life with nothing left behind—a life that was well utilized. A life lived—entirely.

That is the kind of life I want, the kind of life I'm called to—one with a heart fully open and exposed, even if it's intimidating.

Tucking away pieces of myself feels safe, but it is a safety that also cages and guards, not just from loss and heartbreak but from joy and happiness too. Those untouched places seem shielded from ache and melancholy, but they become shielded from authentic relationships and unfiltered influence too.

In trying to create a heart that pain can't penetrate as sharply, I'm also creating a heart emptier of all the things hearts were meant for. I'm unknowingly creating fragmented love and wishfully hoping that pain won't have the ability to find the hidden parts. Because the truth is, pain is powerful, and it's known for finding not only the hidden parts, but pieces that we didn't even know existed because we hadn't met them yet.

What I need is a heart that's brave enough to break, because only then will I be using it the way it was intended.

Love isn't meant to be partial, especially when fragmented by fear.

Hearts aren't designed for portions to remain unused or unfelt or hidden.

Our souls are meant for meaning and our lives are created for purpose.

Entirely.

Grief, pain, and sorrow are all the consequence of openness, of vulnerability. But you can't experience any of those without first experiencing the gift of profound influence and beautiful love.

I no longer intentionally leave open spaces and hidden places. I want to be fully known, fully loved, and eventually, one day, fully remembered.

My heart is open. Is yours?

can't feel their love

I've known heartbreak. I've felt it. I've had guys go from loving me to loving someone else within days, maybe even hours. I've known love unrequited. I've known breakups and even divorce. None of those held the impact of no longer feeling the love of a parent—one stolen by disease and death, a parent no longer here.

There were aspects of grief people warned me about: fear, sorrow, despair. There were insights shared about how I'd feel both orphaned and homeless. All those things were true. Grief is as fickle and powerful as they say.

No one warned me how I'd be breathless the first time I felt the impact of not feeling my mother's love anymore. Not that it wasn't real, or true, but that I would no longer actively feel it being given and certainly that I wouldn't be able to witness it anymore.

I never understood how anyone could feel unlovable, or unloved, until the day my heart started palpitating in a way it never had before. It would skip beats and then beat in double-time, as if it had forgotten its steady repetition. Before I ever did, my body recognized I could no longer feel the most significant person in my life loving me. The parent I was closest with, the one who loved me the most effortlessly, that person was suddenly unable to provide that love.

I believe in heaven and that love never dies. I'm also intelligent enough to know that loving someone earthside is much different than loving someone heavenside. The two cannot be compared, for one is built from observed experience and one is built from hope. Hope is beautiful, but it cannot take the place of something physical and felt in a way that has evidence. One form is tangible, the other invisible and assumed.

Love from heaven is often diminished to coincidence. I don't want coincidence. I want the kind of love that offered hugs and cuddles, no matter my age, knowing that they always provided joy to my inner child and also the woman I am now. The kind of love that made me someone's daughter, someone's kid. I want love that is evident and visible. I want the love that you not only feel but see.

When you wake up and realize that kind of love is no longer a possibility, your heart is changed in ways it never fully recovers from. When I was younger, I had a friend who was born with a hole in her heart. She had multiple surgeries, but we always knew her heart was different, unique. I imagine mine is now the same—imperfect with scars that cannot ever let it be what it once was.

There is no book, no manual, no guidance on how to recover and process the moment you wake up and can no longer feel them loving you. It's a reality of grief that is too harsh to reveal, too brutal to discuss.

No one can love you like a parent, which is what makes their love so dynamic, so needed. That love attaches itself to you before you ever take your first breath, and sadly, the experience of that love leaves when they take their last. You've never known a life without it until the moment they die, and you suddenly do.

There is cherished beauty in the infinity of their love. Yet that fact does not diminish the disappointment and devastation of not being able to feel and witness and experience that love the way you always have—physically, in a manner where they were just as alive as the adoration and pride they produced.

In fresh grief you cannot feel them loving you, even though you know they did. You can no longer see them loving you. You can't experience them loving you. Instead, the only thing you're experiencing is ache and sorrow and fear and anger and all the million things that grief brings with it.

I wait for the day I can feel her loving me again, however God accomplishes that. I'm living inspired by all that she was, and I'm hopeful for the next opportunity I can feel her loving me.

The love they had for us is not gone. It's up to us to start feeling it again because it's there. It's always there, always has been.

stethoscope

I bought a stethoscope after you died. I'd forgotten my own heart was still beating. It seemed impossible. How could a heart still function when grief had damaged it so extensively?

I needed proof.
I had to hear it to believe it.
So, I bought a stethoscope.

And there it was, beating. Broken, but still I heard the steady *thump-thump, thump-thump, thump-thump*.

It felt like a nefarious action, like a betrayal. How can one heart continue to beat when another no longer has that same function, that same capability?

Your heart stopped.
Mine continued.

Grief suddenly made me ashamed of my own body, my own organs, my own life. What had I done to deserve another day when your days were over? What made me worthy of more breaths, more heartbeats?

Is it luck? Is it fate? What decides who stays and who goes?

Is it God? Can I speak with him?

I have questions that cannot be answered and worries with no proper person to contact. I'm holding this medical instrument, wondering how I got here—to a place where I need proof of life, my life.

And instead of running to your grave, stethoscope in hand, chasing hope to see if I can find something, anything, that proves you're still here, that this is all a mistake, I place the cold metal piece back on my chest—and I listen.

Thump-thump.
Thump-thump.
Thump-thump.

And then more—*thump-thump, thump-thump, thump-thump*. Until it softly becomes your voice, and I swear I hear—

This was always my favorite sound, my favorite song. Proof of life. Proof of miracles. Proof of you. Proof of me. When you hear that thump-thump, those precious beats, honor them as evidence of both of us—me then, you now, us always. Hearts stop; love doesn't.

And I cry. And I weep. And I place that stethoscope by my bed for the next time I need a reminder, a proof of life—both yours and mine.

dreams of dying

As a child, I used to wake in the night afraid of death, terrified of it. My screams would alert my mother. Her presence always brought immediate comfort. She'd assure me that I was okay. She'd tell me I had too much time left to worry about death, about dying. She'd say it was far, far away—even though death had just visited only moments ago, still lingering in my mind.

Now, I wake up haunted by her death. Now, it visits when I sleep—both as a replay and as a new tragedy, one built from more horror than truth. I lie in bed and wonder who will calm me from death's nightmares, death's visits. The only one who held that capability now holds the very fate I've been fearful of—gone, dead.

I used to think those dreams, those night terrors, were of my own ending—never hers. Now, I wonder if I feared the wrong ending all along.

Sure, the circle, the cycle, of life tells us that parents go first. What it didn't share, didn't teach, is how it comes on a timeline that doesn't always give gray hair and wrinkles. It comes, ready or not, to take someone you love.

And most nights, just the same, it visits while I sleep. It screams, *Fear me*. And I do. Then it replays my mother's death over and over and over again. Oftentimes adding new endings, new darkness, new drama to compound and compress the already embedded doom, an unrecoverable fate.

And she's always there—dying, the complete opposite of how it was all those years ago. Ironic since back then, she'd comfort me, always fighting death's influence and shadows that filled my mind.

Now the two things are one—death and her.

Tragically combined.

And I wonder who saves you from a nightmare that has become your daytime truth, your sun-risen reality?

I pull out a piece of paper tucked in my nightstand, and I write,

> *Dear Death,*
>
> *You might have come first; your entrance might have been her end. But you were not the final touch, nor the final hand.*
>
> *Just as she came to comfort me, there was someone there for her. He whispered the same soothing words she once whispered to me, words that told her she was okay, she was safe. And she was with him. Just as I was, with her.*
>
> *You might end a life, but God renews a life, not here or with you as a witness—but in heaven. She is in heaven.*
>
> *Death, you have been defeated, you are overcome. Turns out, you aren't so scary when you're not given power and authority that are not your own. So, visit my dreams if you must, but when you do, know that when I wake it won't be you I fear but God I thank.*

Pen down, I go to sleep. And with or without death's nightmares, death's dreams, I'll wake and know that heaven wins. Heaven always wins.

Should one of my children wake one day and tell me they're afraid to die, I'll look at them confidently and say, "You're okay. I've got you. Death is nothing to fear because heaven always wins."

unanswered

I scream at heaven and demand to know why. Heaven isn't like my elementary teachers, where every question is answered, every inquiry is good.

I scream a million questions and cry a hundred more. They go unanswered, always, all of them.

Why this? Why that? Why, why, why?

Why am I tortured with wonderings with no conclusion?

Why are we taught to ask about the fragments in our minds and, even more profound, the longings in our hearts, if one day it will feel as though our voices are silent and our questions unworthy?

My brain was wired for connection, for understanding. I don't understand this. I don't understand death. And maybe that's the entire point, the entire explanation—not having one.

I wonder if death isn't taught in schools because no one has answers for the inevitable questions that would come. In school, people with titles like Mr. or Mrs. held all of the answers, all of the truth. Now, only God does.

And if only God can explain the whys, how do I get my questions to him? Will he be like my teachers—guiding, explaining, instructing? Can he take my whys and soothe them with explanations? Can he listen to my wonderings and resolve their sting, their ache, their confusion?

Faith tells me he can—even a faith that doesn't always feel like mine.

So, I transition my screams to heaven into desperate prayers to God. I plead for him to untangle my whys, to provide a sense of understanding. My prayers end with question marks, and I wonder if prayers are allowed to. I can't seem to frame them any other way.

I pray. I ask why. All at the same time—over and over again. And I hope that his timing will be kinder than my impatience, my confusion. And I wonder if the unanswered prayers people speak about are really unanswered questions, asked through prayer—one and the same. And maybe one day, like certain unanswered prayers, I'll be grateful to never have received the answers. Until then, I'll ask anyway.

I keep asking anyway.

terrified of tomorrow

She was terrified of the empty room—the one that held finality, the one that held death, and harsher even, welcomed it. This room, the room where her mother died, intimidated her in ways that intimately tugged at her heart and mind. She would pass it quickly, always looking down. She'd avoid that area of the house completely if entering wasn't required, but most of the time it was required.

She did the same thing in hospitals, especially the delicate few that held the death of people she knew. There were certain places and spaces that scared her, not for what they could hold but for what they already had—the final breaths and heartbeats of someone she loved.

She was scared of the places where life ended. She wondered if the profound grief of these spaces might snatch her life too.

She was terrified of doctors' appointments and opening test results on computer screens. She feared health in new ways. She feared routine appointments and annual exams. She wondered if others did too. She held back tears nearly every time she stepped foot in any kind of health facility—hospitals, doctors' offices—the anxiety and trepidation did not discriminate.

She feared death so intensely that it sometimes felt as if the anxiousness of it all was a thief—just like she always knew death itself to be. In fact, she wondered if the fear of death might hold a harsher impact and demise than death itself. After all, death leads to heaven. Anxiety and fear have only led to emptied joy and scattered resolve.

She was scared of life, or rather, of losing life—sometimes hers and sometimes the lives of everyone she loved. She wanted to stay, and she wanted them to stay too. Every choice she made was based on not only survival and love but also fear. Her mind made calculations and predictions as if it were suddenly a scientist or a mathematician. She had never been either or anything close. Fear gave her new skills. None of them worthy or beneficial.

She was terrified of both being alone and leaving the little ones who loved her alone too. She prayed both out of desperation and out of hope. She grieved the same. She possibly loved the same too.

She held on to things she didn't need and let go of things she assumed no longer kept her safe. She began to ignore things that were gifted only with longevity. She watched too many people she loved die before inheriting their own investments. Some hadn't even made it to gray hair and old age.

They never got to retire. Would she?

She is uneasy about that answer.

She prays for yes. Fear keeps whispering *no*.

She is scared of things beyond her control and fearful of things she cannot manipulate or mold. Yet still, she tries. Sometimes through prayer, sometimes through proactivity. Always through worry, and sometimes also through panic.

She has an aversion to cemeteries, not because they hold the bodies of those she loves but because it's the place that will eventually hold her body. A place that silently screams—*death, death, death.*

She wishes grief hadn't made her this way, afraid. She thinks about the shell she has become. She can see the change death has had on her. She can feel the transformations grief has led to.

She is different—so, so different.

And with time, through fear and worry and anxiousness, she realizes that maybe survival isn't about avoiding the empty room but learning to stand in it. It isn't about being fearful of her health but proactively participating and choosing knowledge over naivety. She cannot change what will happen in that room. She will never know what each tomorrow holds.

She knows fear will never fully leave her. She thinks maybe it shouldn't. She can carry multiple things at once. In fact, she always has. And maybe that is enough to keep entering spaces and experiences she once avoided, and to allow herself, slowly, to hope again.

She wants to find hope again.

grief as a casket

He has the audacity to say, "We did not bury you, so why do you act gone too, confined to grief like it's a casket?"

And I wonder how his grief doesn't feel like a casket. I wonder how he doesn't feel just as "gone" as I do, just as "gone" as the body we've buried.

He stands judging my brokenness and sorrow as if he shouldn't be carrying the same load, the same devastation. Is he better at hiding it or does he genuinely not feel wrapped in the heaviness of grief, the chaos of losing someone irreplaceable?

No, I haven't been buried but that doesn't mean I don't feel the weight of six feet of dirt or the claustrophobia of a life enclosed in wood—forever.

I'd love to know his secrets, his remedies. Is it denial? Because my brain won't let me forget this grave truth. Is it strength? Is it faith? Is it something in his DNA that I didn't inherit?

For me, grief *is* a casket—a tomb that holds all of my "what ifs" and "wish I would haves." A place that holds all of my *why? why? whys?*

Grief is the placeholder for them, someone I love, someone I miss.

You know what's worse than an empty seat? A seat that is now occupied by grief instead of a person, your person.

Why must I hold loss and grief and also the expectation that it cannot be seen or witnessed by others? Why does my grief get judged instead of wrapped in sympathy and compassion?

Grief is a casket. It's a place the world confines us also so that they aren't faced with the harsh realities of life—so they aren't forced to see that death exists and people die. And consequently people live, like me, with loss and death's truth.

They don't realize loss gave me grief, but the world gave me a casket.

A place to hide the visible pain.

A place to confine and conceal heartbreak and sorrow and despair.

A place to retreat so that they can live without the reminder that grief exists, that it lives.

Grief is like a casket.
A box to hold all of my shattered pieces.
A tomb for all the things that can no longer be.
A shelter for the heartbreak the world cannot bear to see.

And I wonder why he doesn't have one, why he isn't confined to his own casket of grief. And I'll probably never know, because I'm confined to this casket the world calls grief.

something new

"I exist differently in the world without her—my mother."

xox, Chels

the stranger who is you

The stranger you see in the mirror is you. I hope one day you'll love her. I hope one day you'll realize how much she endures yet continues.

I hope you look at her with a lens of beauty and pride. A lens you never apply to yourself—a lens you use only for others.

This stranger you see, she deserves to be appreciated.
She deserves to be seen.
She deserves to be known.

You need to get to know her. After all, *she is you*.

She will remain an outsider, an unknown soul, an unrecognized face until you let her in. Until you greet her in a way you would a loved one at the airport—anticipating and awaiting her arrival. Grateful she exists—because again, *she is you*.

You exist still, through pain, through grief, through mourning, and through sorrow. You exist through her, a woman who has experienced immeasurable suffering, yet prevails.

You are her, this stranger is you.

This unknown woman, this unfamiliar face, this stranger you see is you—transformed by things out of her control but also transformed by greatness. Your greatness. Their greatness. A legacy's greatness. A combined eminence.

Love her.
Accept her.
Heal with her.

The stranger in the mirror is you—the current and transformed you.

Please don't keep her a stranger for long. You've both survived too much, too long to remain strangers.

that part of yourself

You're never going to find that part of yourself again—the part that seemed to evaporate when grief and pain came along. I know you long for it. I know you search for it, but it's no longer yours. You've been changed by heartbreak, and you've been wounded in ways that can never fully heal.

You will be different now—both in ways you welcome and in ways you despise.

Time will be your greatest gift for renewal and healing, but it will also be the thing that you fear the most—knowing it's borrowed, and you don't know when it will run out—because you've seen it run out prematurely and unexpectedly.

That part of yourself that you're aching for, the one that you cannot seem to find—it isn't coming back. You can search for it as desperately and as intently as you search for the beautiful person you've lost—both are gone forever. I wish I could tell you losing this person, and this significant piece of yourself, gets easier—it does not. But it does get different.

Instead of counting the holes and being overwhelmed by the void, consider this a new version of you. Not a broken and shattered and irreparable you but one who is a work in progress, a zone of rebuild—pieced together by things that cannot fade, things like love.

The version of you that existed before witnessing death, before standing in a room that experienced one less heartbeat than before, that version is gone. But I promise you, this new version is worthy of added days and years and moments.

This version of you will end up more beautiful than the one before, inside and out, because this version will mean more. It will be built from pain and from wisdom. It will be built from loss, but also from a legacy. This version of yourself will show you the feeling and meaning of words like grit and strength and resiliency. Words you've grown to detest over the years, but words that you will become—words you're already becoming.

You can't see it yet, but I can. I stood where you're standing years ago, counting empty spaces rather than memories. Counting moments unable to be fulfilled instead of celebrating the memories I was blessed with. Time doesn't erase pain, but it grants you perspective. It grants you the ability to look past grief's wounds and the absence of someone you love and instead feel the blessing of a love and a relationship that transcends everything, even death.

And while it may sound cruel or insensitive to tell you that yes, you lost pieces of yourself you cannot get back, I can tell you confidently that in time, this new version of yourself is a blend of you and them—which is the best version you could ever be.

This version of you was ripped apart and huge holes were chiseled into the spaces where you were once whole. But it's only because the space was needed to braid all that they were and all that they will be through you, right inside of you—living on, forever.

In time, when you've been blessed by healing's perspective, I hope you see that this version is the best one. It's you and them together—two legacies, one left behind to be cherished and one that is still in the making.

This version of you needed the empty spaces first, so it could make what you've become—part them but still you too. I can't wait for you to appreciate and admire this incomparable version of you.

a life built around you

My entire life was built around you, every step, every milestone—each piece, both the beautiful and the broken. Because of that, things shattered and became unrecognizable when you died. It's hard to imagine life without the center stone, without you.

My life was built around you from the start, both by nature and by our design. One day I woke up and the life built with your guidance had been completely redesigned. How can a life still exist and still continue without its core, without its foundation?

When you're left with death's wreckage and grief's debris, you're forced to assess the damage, collect the rubble, and eventually rebuild. There is no other choice. Outsiders call this strength; insiders call this survival. I know strength and resiliency exist, but I often wonder how they are found or if, instead, they are gifted to a lucky few.

After losing you, I became afraid of change because change seemed cruel. Change meant becoming a stranger in my own life, with holes left by an absence that death created—your death. Usually, you'd be the one I'd seek in moments like this, but now that option has vanished, lost to time or lack thereof.

How does one adapt and recover from someone so significant being physically eliminated from their life? Is it time or therapy? Is it from death itself? Or is it from accepting and acknowledging the changes that must take place to keep experiencing life's beauty and wonder?

Change is inevitable, and yet I'm suddenly terrified of it. I'm fearful of becoming a version of myself that you don't know, which really means a version that you've never loved. I'm afraid of change because who I was just days ago feels like both a complete stranger and also someone I want to find with the same desperation I wish I could find you again.

My life was built around you and now it feels as if what once was permanent is now mobile and quickly venturing to a location I am not familiar with, nor want. Some say that death is a change of worlds, but isn't grief too? Grief's world shifts from *with them* to *without them*, such a harsh variation.

My entire life has been built around you, every step, every milestone—all pieces, both the beautiful and the broken. The challenge now seems to be finding a way to build without the original base—you—while still ensuring that you are a significant designer of the rebuild.

And as I contemplate what this unique and forced remodel will look like, I realize that before, when you were here, my life wasn't built around you but *with* you.

Now is the moment, the opportunity, my life begins being built around you—around your love, your memory, and your influence. Around your unforgettability. Around your inspiration and your faith. Around your beauty and your hope. Around all of the pieces that I cherished, which is really all of them.

On my hard days I will accept that the challenge is to keep building, to keep adding to my life by using all you gave me, the greatest being the resiliency of love and the strength found in that truth.

Lives get built with those we love, until one day we inherit the ability to start building our lives around them. That is what a legacy is, it's loving someone with an unwavering promise to keep their memory alive by living boldly and beautifully in their honor.

I'll no longer be afraid of change because this change will be led by me and inspired by you.

It's both an opportunity and a treasure to have a life built around you.

how has this loss changed you?

I'm sitting on a stage being interviewed. The audience is gazing at me as if they see a grief expert. I'm not. I'm simply a woman who has lost people she loves and written about the experience. I'm not even sure I believe experts on grief exist. Grief is something so unique, so specially tethered to the relationship and the lives it was attached to, it seems the only experts are us. Outsiders, even those who have experienced the death of someone significant, can't possibly know all of the intricacies and specificities to the absence you're left with and the transformations that occur without your consent, unique to you and you alone.

Most everyone in the room already has tears in their eyes, me included. The microphone raises to the interviewer, softly she says, "How has this loss changed you?" I pause to catch my breath. It's impossible to respond to a question when the answer is still unfolding.

I cannot measure or count the ways this loss has changed me, for grief's limit does not exist.

Grief has shifted and manipulated every portion of my being and every space of my life. It has changed how I interact and also how I respond. It has changed the way I speak and also the manner in which I listen. It has changed each crevice of who I thought I was and each revision of who I will become. It has dulled the sharp edges that I used to hold, some of which were created by loss itself.

How do you measure change? How do you count the blocks of a rebuild when they're being glued back together, shard by shard, not brick by brick? How do you calculate a heart's resilience and a soul's pain?

I'm confident that I haven't yet comprehended the depths of grief's changes and transformations because no matter how many years it has been, the adjustments continue to come. I'm not sure grief ever ceases to mold and blend and weave together both present and past things in new ways—ways that make you feel unrecognizable in both devastating and breathtaking ways.

Grief changes you forever.

Instead of asking how this loss *has* changed me, I think it's easier to identify how this loss *hasn't* changed me. That answer is simple.

It hasn't changed the titles that bonded us together, titles like mother and daughter. It may have changed the space between, split by earthside and heaven, but it has not changed the fact that she loved me and I loved her. In fact, love present tense because love persists, always. It hasn't changed her impact or her influence; in fact, it has solidified it.

Profound loss changes you in ways you cannot express and in versions that you haven't met yet, for they are still being drafted, curated. The powerful thing about this question is *in what way* you will let it change you.

Will you become more compassionate or more ruthless? Will you let the changes be drawn by love or by heartbreak? Will you let grief change you by gratitude for what was or by the anger for what will never be? Will you be changed through patience and grace, allowing time to heal and process? Or will you be quick to cover and hide the realities of death's consequences on the living?

When I finally compose myself enough to look into the audience and answer the question, I say: "Let's not ask how this loss has changed us, but rather, how we will work to ensure the changes are created not only by unimaginable loss but also by unwavering love. Let us not give the power to grief alone but instead work as cocreators for what will be. The new versions of ourselves should not be defined by one thing but rather a collaboration between all things—both the blessings and the burdens. We are not powerless in this change, in this shift. We must remember this on our hardest days. We are more than the sum of our losses and our lives should be empowered by that truth. Grief's changes are inevitable. Love's changes must be chosen, deliberately utilized. My hope is that each one of us walks away freshly inspired to be a catalyst for change with just as much command as grief. The question now becomes, Will we?"

And now, each day I ask myself, *How will I allow this loss to change me?* And the answer is always, **with love**.

trying to remember me

I'm trying to remember me, who I am, who I was. This death seems to have me confused, like an emotional and unstable adolescent who doesn't know her purpose and hasn't quite found her worth, her grounding.

I know I can't pick up the millions of pieces that grief has seemed to break me into, but also, I can't remember what most of them were. I have no clue how to try and find them. Too many. Too broken. Too small. Too forgotten.

I'm trying to find who I was so I can use it to shape who I will be, but I fear that version of me is buried underneath the ground, farther than the six feet the dead have been placed. How do you find something when you can't recall its shape or its form? How do you find something that feels like it never existed?

Maybe instead of finding, I should be forming—me.
Me after death, not mine but theirs.

Maybe I should be formulating and drafting the next version, the one that must come. One with the fearless goal to make them proud. Their life should be the inspiration behind the newness to come. Their love should be the guide and the cocreator.

I shouldn't be working to find past versions that no longer exist, though I am. I should be using my energy, conserving my energy, for the rebuild, the remake. Not by choice but by my command or rather demand. Grief's demand.

The dead whisper, “Say you'll remember me.” My old self doesn't. Maybe the goal was always to lose her, me. Maybe the plan was always for grief and loss to transition me to something new.

I'll surrender. I'll give up the hunt. I'll let this death do what it came to do. I will be open to its lessons and accepting of its changes. Hoping that is the right thing. What is the real right thing?

I'll remember them, not me. I'll save my memory for their greatness, not all of the things I've been separated from.

I'll use each compartment in my mind to reminisce on what remains.

Their love. Their influence. Their wisdom. Their legacy.

In some ways pieces of them have outlived pieces of me.

Ironically, that feels just and fair.

Maybe at first you forget yourself so you can never forget them. That's a trade I'm willing to make, a swap I can live with. If the choice is to remember them or the old version of me, I choose them.

Say you'll remember—and it will be them.

I'll always remember them; we'll always remember them.

Some things can never be forgotten.

One day in my final version, the one that's seen its completion, I hope I become one of them. For now, it's them, always them.

the night we met

The night we met I was too numb, too shocked, to know you had even arrived. I was too busy fixating on the body being physically removed from the house that I was in and all of the things that would also be lost by that harsh reality.

I was too heartbroken to see anything beyond an empty space, an empty bed.

I was too focused on slowing the anxiety to realize that as her last breath slipped away, you snuck in, uninvited. Instantaneously death came and so did you.

The night we met no one named you, nor did they introduce us in a manner that would show your significance.

Grief. *Your name is grief.*

You're the kind of guest that doesn't require an invitation, nor a welcoming. For if you did, you'd never be here. No one wants your presence, your dominance. Your harshness. No one wants you.

Instead, they want the one who was taken, the one who died. They want to undo the opportunity that allowed you to exist, to come. I'd ask why you exist, but sadly, this is life. Death is the universal outcome. You are the universal consequence of that unavoidable truth.

You are grief.

You are so many harsh and brutal things. Others explained to me that at your core you are love. I had to wait to learn that version of you. Like a friend that starts as a foe, you were feared. You were disliked and suspicious. You were hostile, at least in my eyes. You were possibly misunderstood, but only because of the confidence and intensity that you arrived with.

You came like an emotional whiplash—a sudden burst of pain, an injury.

You walked in like you already knew the place, like you already knew the people. You came in sneaky and obscure. You came as grief. You came as you, unafraid and persistent.

With time I learned your roots, your whys, your intentions. You started to fit in. You started to be part of the plan, the purpose. I started to see that while you didn't arrive gently, you arrived *needed.*

Needed so we could process the pain. *Needed* so we could learn from the outcome. *Needed* so we could heal. *Needed* for a million reasons we still have yet to learn. *Needed* to inspire and encourage the change that was inevitable.

And as I changed, so did you. Eventually we both became something new. You, love. Me, a legacy.

I'm different because of your influence and you are different because of my willingness to see all facets of your being.

The day we met, you were only grief, and I was only broken. Now, we are different. We are a togetherness of both harsh and wondrous things. We are blended. We are one.

You came as grief, inevitable.
And now we are both something new.
You, love. Me, a legacy.

what will become of me

Wait and see what will become of me, not now but eventually, when the weight of grief is lighter and the avalanche of their death has done all of the damage it will do. Just wait, because what will become of me will be something powerful, something magical, even though I don't believe in magic. At least, not yet. But trust me, wait until you see what becomes of me, because something will.

Not only because of this loss, this hole, but in honor of it.

I will become something from all of this, and it will be meaningful.

It has to be meaningful—for them, and for me. But mostly for them, or maybe for the ones that look to me with loving eyes and seek hope and faith and guidance. The ones who call me wife or mother or friend.

I will become something new from all of this.

It will be built by tragedy but molded by an influence this world was lucky to have. Yes, have. That influence isn't present anymore, but that doesn't mean it's not remembered. And certainly, it doesn't mean that it doesn't extend in fresh ways that go beyond a grave and an obituary—a death.

One day when the grief has lifted and the healing begins, I will become something. Something different than before because the version I used to be has been lost, just like the person I loved, the person that loved me—one lost to eternity, one lost to pain.

I am determined to become something new from all of this.

Wait and see what will become of me when I can breathe freer again, when my day shifts from being filled with tears and ache into gratitude and contentment. When I spend more time anywhere but the bathroom floor or the ground of the cemetery. When I rise, and keep rising, refusing to fall to the depths that loss and mourning led me. And I will rise. Not today, but someday.

One day I will become something, a woman different in ways that matter. Changed in ways that multiply goodness, and ways that acknowledge the harshness of heartbreak while not allowing it power or leadership. I will use my brokenness to bend and flex in new ways, ways that allow me to live with more intention and more ambition. Ways that remind me to boldly live because living is a privilege.

I will become something new from all of this because they matter and life matters, and when you're the only one with the freedom and ability to keep living, you must.

I must keep living.

And I will, because eventually, I will become something new from all of this.

I will become their memory keeper, their memory sharer. I will rise from grief through the brilliant influence and motivation of remembrance and honor, the honor to ensure the only thing gone is their body—everything else from their name to their smile will remain, treasured and alive. Alive in ways they can't be.

I will become something new from all of this.

A legacy. I will become a legacy.

And you will too. You will too.

bird's nest

Birds have built a nest in the wreath of my front door. They happily sing a melody as they build in a space that I thought was mine. They're too joyful for me to scare away, so I let them build. I let them create.

It starts with twigs and then leaves and bark. Each hour, each day, it gets a bit bigger, a bit more structured and secure. I stare in amazement of their work. They've taken tiny scraps and turned it into something safe, something they'll call home.

They've taken feathers and sticks, yarn and even small pieces of fabric. They've taken scraps and trash and remnants of things and built something from it—their nest, their safe space.

That is grief.

Having nothing. Being left with nothing but shattered pieces, torn parts, scraps of everything that remains, and being forced to build something with it. To accept that *what was* can never be and the only way to make *what will be* is to build it.

Build from the rubble. Build from the devastation. Build from the remaining fragments, because in grief, there are only fragments. Nothing remains whole. Nothing complete.

It's as if these birds are trying to teach me a lesson on resilience and grit. As if they're trying to show me that meaningful and necessary things can be built from debris, built from wreckage. They've created something from the brokenness of things, something from things so tiny others viewed them as worthless or disposable.

For these birds, the brokenness holds potential. It holds the foundation for the very space that they'll use to experience flight.

They started with nothing. They had to collect each piece, each tiny fragment.

And with effort and purpose and intentionality, they used the rubble, jagged pieces and all, to form the very space that will hold them safely.

Ever think that maybe we're called to do the same?

Maybe we're called to build again, to create again, so eventually all of those pieces become the foundation for what's next. Maybe we're called to collect the shattered pieces and use them in new ways, making a space that, at first, keeps us safe, and then one day, becomes the very space that encourages us to fly, to soar—to live.

Brokenness isn't an end. It's the material we will use to ensure their life stays *memorable* and ours stays *livable*.

If birds can so freely and authentically see brokenness as potential, why can't we?

she sees kindness, not grief

My daughter holds up a shirt while we're shopping. "Mom, look! This shirt is you!" The shirt reads *Do everything with kindness*. She's already moved on to the next rack of clothes as I, for the first time, realize this version of me—one that is imperfect and etched with heartbreak—must be okay. This version must be doing something right to get a comment like this, especially from her—a teenager.

Grief came and immediately started crafting transformations. In the fresh and early days those changes were dark and uncomplimentary. They stole so much of me—my light and my hope the most critical of them all. With time, grief's edits, grief's makeovers, were still dramatic and created by a power higher than my own, but they were less harmful and more purposeful. The changes were never just physical, though in the beginning, loss changed my face and form as much as the rest.

The most monumental changes were internal. They were deeper than surface level and undoubtedly happening without my consent or authorship. Grief alone was the creator of each version of me following profound loss. I am a combination of both life's and grief's transformations.

And until now, until this very moment, I had always assumed this was an unfortunate thing—a very harsh and unfortunate thing.

Seeing myself through my daughter's eyes, a woman she has observed and decided is built from kindness, is a woman I am proud of.

This constantly healing and delicately torn version isn't quite the brittle and disastrous version I had envisioned or created in my mind. Death did not eliminate the influence of someone spectacular; it illuminated it—in me.

This version, the one my daughter recognized before I did, is one I should appreciate and admire. It's a version that holds empty spaces but doesn't collapse into them. It's a version who stares at the name of someone I love on a headstone while never turning to stone myself. It's the version who holds a "minus one" while knowing there are still a million positives to count too. This version of me lives through grief each day, not making it my personality while still allowing it to be part of my newfound purpose.

This version of me should be celebrated, not undervalued because of shame or the world's expectations.

We become so many different versions of ourselves in life. Grief seems to speed up and amplify those processes, sometimes even multiplying the number of versions we have. In the beginning I was scared to become something new, something and someone my deceased loved one would never know. It felt like betrayal. Now, it feels like a calling to keep becoming, recognizing with each new me that I'm more healed, more patient, more kind, and more aware of the things to value in life.

How can I regret or despise a version of me seen as a woman built from kindness? Especially when that kindness came from someone I admire and miss.

Grief edits and it transforms. It chisels and it erases, and you change, version after version, until one day you're the best you can be.

And I'm not there yet. But for now, I'll be proud of the woman my daughter sees, and I hope one day I realize it's me.

death is a door

Why would I fear death when death is the door that leads you to heaven?

Death seemed so much scarier, so much more intimidating, when it wasn't the portal that delivered me to you.

Death used to seem like a dark pit, like a black hole of unknowns. Now, death is tied to you, tied to heaven in new ways. It's the same name, the same title, the same reality, but a new perspective of fate and finality.

How can I fear anything attached to you? How can I fear any outcome you were worthy of? How can I worry about any place or destination where you reside, or at the very least passed through?

Death used to be a shadow that came to steal the people I love. Hope taught me that instead, death is a guide, a chaperone, that leads to God, to heaven, to forever.

Death was unnerving when it felt like a thief, like an endless abyss, like an end, like a placement of eternal nothingness.

But death is a door—
an opening to heaven.
an invitation from God.
a reuniting with you.

Death is the thing I feared most in the world until I learned it's the door that leads to everything I've been searching for—

you.
God.
heaven.
eternity.

One day when death's door opens for me, I'll see you and you'll lead me toward everything that matters—an arrival in forever, with you, with everyone.

Death is a door.

hope

"In these moments of heartbreaking grief,
I remember that the only reason we have an empty space
is because we were blessed with someone who loved us
so beautifully, it occupied an entire part of our soul."

xox, Chels

message of hope

You've sunk into a sea of sorrow and you're searching for a message of hope. I can see it in your eyes, even though you're trying to hide it. I can tell your body is aching for comfort and peace just as strongly as it aches for the person you've lost. You don't feel hope anymore, but you want to.

You're silently searching for a message of hope—for a message that healing after loss is possible.

You're drenched in the weight of grief, yet deep down, you're silently praying for the world to give you a sign that you'll be okay. Just like your person used to tell you, used to promise, that you will, in fact, be okay.

You hold a new, bolder empathy and a sharp, invisible pain, but you want to hold hope too. You wonder if the world will feel safe and worthy and worthwhile again. You wonder if strength is just an illusion and healing is just a trend, something people work toward but never actually achieve. You wonder if fear has replaced contentment, and sadness has replaced everything else. You wonder, *If hope exists, where is it?*

What you can't see is that it's there, waiting. Waiting for the moment you're truly ready for it. Waiting for the moment that it can be welcomed instead of pushed away. You see, hope doesn't leave, but it tucks itself away, hidden, in order to let grief's lessons and wisdom do their powerful, yet delicate, job. It waits for the realities of loss to set in and for the truths of death to be revealed. It waits for your mind to comprehend all the things you're running from, all of the leftovers scattered from heartbreak and unexpected and unwanted life lessons.

Hope never leaves, it simply shares the space with other emotions, experiences, and truths so that when it shines again, you appreciate it with an intensity you could have never held before. It waits until it is welcomed, not forced upon you. It waits until you are ready, which is different for each person who has experienced loss.

Hope waits because it knows its power and its influence, and it also knows the power of letting grief's impact have value and influence too. Grief and loss shape us, sure, by harsh and complicated ways but also by ways that lead to creating legacies and living fuller than ever before. Grief can often open new passions, new places of advocacy and drive, that only personally experiencing the fragility of life can provide.

Both hope and grief are masterminds of impactful outcomes, one more likable than the other, but both profound and important.

Hope is there and you will be okay, though both will look different than before. When your heart is ready and your soul and mind are too, hope will reveal itself again. It will shine and it will light the way for all that is to come. Because for you, there is more to come, and it's beautiful.

in the waiting

At first, I believed grief when it told me death meant *gone forever*. I believed the harshness and the infinity in that statement. I believed the lies of heartbreak and the deceit of loss. I let grief chisel away all of the pieces of hope and love. I let the weight of loneliness and disbelief lessen optimism.

I trusted grief when it said death meant gone forever.

I trusted grief when it said their influence and their love would not last.

I trusted grief when it said physical absence is more potent and superior than an invisible presence.

I trusted grief when it said that the weight of six feet of dirt should be felt not only by the one buried but also by me.

I trusted grief.

Over and over again, I trusted grief.

I held the *gone forever* until it nearly stole more than the life that had already been taken. I held it until it shattered my joy and broke my dreams for anything beyond the moments that already were—the past. I held it until it became my inner voice, my place of decision-making, and my influence on how things would be moving forward. I held on to the deception of *gone forever* instead of the brilliance of *goodbye for now*.

I believed grief when it came and said, *the end*. I wish I would have been brave enough to challenge that thought and that perspective. I wish I would have been opposed to any option that signified anything other than a pause, a waiting.

That is what death is—a waiting, one waiting earthside, the other heavenside.

There is no *gone forever*, there is only gone momentarily. Grief should not be trusted in its harshest moments. It should be acknowledged and listened to when the sting has lightened and the weight has decreased. It should be a partner with things, not a dictator. It should be an acknowledgment of *what no longer is* while still honoring the hope of *what will eventually be* and the gratitude for *what already was*.

Grief is proof of love. It is a receipt for a life lived, now missed. It is an invisible certificate of the heart that signifies and solidifies a relationship—a connection with the resiliency to extend beyond lungs with breath and lungs without. Grief is love at its final stage—the final stage before the endless reunion, before heaven.

If grief feels like despair and hopelessness, if it feels like only darkness and mourning, you're in the waiting—grief's waiting.

With time, grief's waiting shifts from emptiness to reminiscence and from loneliness to a beautiful companion of influence and inherited legacies.

Instead of trusting grief, I now trust the waiting.

I trust the momentary pause of presence on this side of heaven in hopes of eventually exchanging it for an infinite reuniting.

Earth has limits. Heaven doesn't. So, for now, I trust the waiting.

my younger self

Last night, I saw an old picture of myself. I was twenty and tan and still naive to the pain of the world. I recognized the background and the outfit, but I barely recognized the girl who was smiling back at me.

We are two different versions, her and I.
She is me in the before—
Before the death of someone irreplaceable.
Before the heartbreak of a forever absence.
Before grief.

I study the picture, trying to soak up how it used to feel to be her, the younger version, the version that didn't know the heart-break of death.

I can't help but internalize how beautiful she is. She's stunning but she never saw it. I think for the first time I am looking at her (and me) through my mother's eyes. Through the lens of love and purity and time. Through the lens of truth that sometimes oneself cannot see, especially in the moment, the present. I now understand why my mother's eyes would sparkle when she smiled at me—it was love, effortless and unwavering love, and probably pride too.

If only I could make a wish and bring the youthful version of myself to life, the one from the picture I hold. I want to talk to her. I want to tell her things. I want to listen as she talks about our mother. I want to remember. I love remembering. She has no idea that our mother will never make it past the age of fifty-seven, and worse, no idea that our mother will die.

One day, when she becomes me, our mom will be only a memory.

I wish I could tell her so many things, the biggest being to cherish our mother—every moment, every minute. I wish I could tell her how healing it will be to know we've never taken our mother for granted. I wish I could gently hug her and tell her it's that truth that will carry us when we're weighed down from the grief of losing her. Our mother taught us to love boldly and with intentional purpose, which will be the invisible salve that will heal grief's sharp cuts and chiseled holes.

I wish I could tell her she's beautiful—our mother's daughter.

I wish I could tell her I'm still learning and growing and in a constant pursuit to make our mother proud from heaven, something she started. I wish I could tell her to walk life with gratitude and to love with intentionality, even quicker than our mother is encouraging her to do now. Maybe if she works faster and more fiercely, I won't hold as much regret—we won't hold as much regret, since she is, after all, just me.

I wish I could go back to her, just for a day, where I'm *still in the experiencing* and *not in the remembering*. I wish things and people were just as alive as they were then, in that moment. I wish I knew them more intimately, like her, instead of only as memories.

I wish.
I wish.
I wish.

But I am not her. I am grown—too grown to believe in birthday-candle wishes and pennies-in-a-fountain hopes. Too grown to believe in time machines or technology that can switch her and me, if even for a moment. I am me, the current version of us, the one in the now. I'm the one grateful for both this version, the one that survives with messy grit and fickle strength, and the one who grieves not being her version anymore.

She is me, with a mother.
I am her, without a mother.
She is *only her*, but I am *both of us*.

So, I will grieve for both of us. And I will live for both of us. And I will *become* something for both of us—I will become my mother's legacy, our mother's legacy. And together, both this young girl from the photo and I, both versions of my mother's daughter, will build something beautiful.

Will you allow both versions of you, both the version *with* and the version *without*, to do the same?

still counting blessings

They'd want us to keep counting our blessings. They'd want our life to be weighed not by hardships and loss but by the gifts of influence, love, and added days. They'd want us to look into the details, not with disdain or with a scorned soul but with a heart open to see the intricate design of goodness.

They'd want us to be listing our blessings before our disappointments. And they'd be confident that when we did, we'd be counting higher and higher for all of life's gifts, and they'd be even more assured that our list of sorrows and catastrophes would be heavy but not forever. Their hope would be for us to tire before we could ever find a number high enough to represent our precious offerings and inheritance.

They knew that grief and sadness would be part of our experience, but they'd be optimistic that it wouldn't be the center of it. They knew that regret would fill our minds, but they'd be hopeful that it wouldn't fill our hearts. They knew that we would miss them, but they'd be confident of the camouflaged ways of coincidence in which their presence would be gently held.

They lived too, remember? They knew pain and loss and grief and death too. And still, they counted blessings. They counted life's goodness while holding life's messiness, which is what they'd want for us too.

So, are we? Are we counting blessings or are we drowning in the unfair and the unjust? Are we able to see the honor of holding a legacy beyond our own or are we overwhelmed by the responsibility of it? Are we able to not only miss them, yearn for them, but also be driven and empowered by them?

Grief comes and we suddenly lose both the desire and the capability to count our blessings, to recognize the good that still exists—because it does still exist. Losing someone important is like having the lights go out—pitch-black, in the middle of an important task. You cannot see. You feel lonely and fearful, desperately wanting light again, vision again, safety again.

In grief, finding light and hope and a newfound purpose can feel like a solo journey.

It's challenging to have a grateful heart when that same heart has been ripped open, severed with gaping holes that sting from death's aftermath. It's hard to find appreciation when all you feel is agony and abandonment. It's difficult to comprehend the blessings that remain when the most noticeable things are the deep voids and the unfillable spaces that arrived when someone we loved became a name carved in stone—gone, forever.

Death isn't a choice. Grief isn't a choice. **Gratitude is a choice.**

In the aftermath of life's messiness, you must choose gratitude.

Are you?

Death finds you. Grief finds you. But you have to find gratitude.

In the fallout of loss, you have to seek gratitude. You have to search for it—again and again and again. Are you?

When they were alive, they did—they counted life's goodness and wonders until they couldn't count anymore. Sometimes aloud, most of the time silent. And did you know, you were always first on the list—the priceless gift they cherished most. They told everyone. The whole world knew. Back then, you knew too. Do you still?

You were named a blessing, a gift. You were counted as something adored and treasured. Now, here without them, can you be bold enough to count your blessings—instead of only being recognized as one? Can you be courageous enough to look into the details of your life, still unfolding, and see beauty and love and gifts?

Start counting. Start with them. They can still, and will always, be a blessing—near or far, earthside or in heaven. And I imagine, they're looking down and thinking, *I hope she's still counting her blessings. I am—now more than ever.*

May we never let grief steal our recognition of what is good, and may we live, both counting our blessings and being one—just as they'd want us to.

seen like that

How she saw me is gone. No one will ever look at me with the same lens, the same love. I lost that when she died—the ability to be seen and known through her, by her.

It's more than just the way her eyes always glistened of love, even when disappointed. It's more than just the way she would calm me with a touch before anyone else could even sense my anxiety or worry. It's more than just the way she would laugh at my dramatics and emotional unsteadiness in a way that grounded me before I ever had the chance to lose control.

All of those things are now gone, now lost, and they cannot be taught or transferred to anyone. She was never taught. She simply inherited the knowing—my knowing.

It's a quiet ache to realize that no one in this world will know and understand me like she did.

Yes, I am loved.
Yes, I am seen.
Yes, I am known and understood.
But no longer by her, no longer in *her* cherished ways.
No longer through her love, her lens.

I know that her love transcends death and heaven and all of the in-between, but that doesn't dissipate the ache to be seen again through her eyes, through her love and adoration.

When she died, I prayed for every single piece of that back, for her back. I used to beg for her. I used to plead for her love, her view, her care, and her understanding. Those prayers, I realized, were hopeless wishes, childish and immature dreams.

Now, grasping reality, planted in truth, instead I pray,

> *Let me see myself as she did—with grace and compassion and not through the magnifying glass zoomed in on my imperfections like I so often do.*
>
> *Let me love myself the way she did—effortless, limitless, and without conditions.*
>
> *Let me know myself the way she did—and then let me appreciate that woman.*
>
> *Let me become my best self—influenced by her life, not her death.*
>
> *Let me, please let me—live beautifully in her honor and her memory.*

No one else will see or love or understand us in the ways they once did—but we can.

And I hope from now on you will, and I hope from now on I will too.

better place

You stand in all black, grief-stricken and bewildered, as person after person shares their condolences and also the sentiments of a *better place*, a place everyone seems to be more hopeful of than you. You cannot begin to comprehend this *better place* and, in fact, despise it more and more each time you hear about it, each time it is mentioned.

"Don't worry, they're in a better place."

"Smile, they're in a better place."

"Rejoice and be grateful, they're no longer in pain, they're in a **better place**."

A better place.

A better place.

A better place.

You hear it over and over and over again.

And you wonder about this *better place*, where it is and what it looks like. You assume they speak of heaven, but no one ever uses that description, that word. You wonder if they did, if your reaction might be softer—more open, more hopeful.

The *best place*, you think, is the one right beside you, the one that now remains empty.

That is the place they should be—here, alive, with you.

You wonder if these people, those not so impacted by this loss, see something you cannot see and feel something you cannot feel.

So, you seek their understanding and the image that they see. You plead for the intuition of the "better place" they know, the one they keep speaking of.

You close your eyes, and you envision this better place, only not as some faraway land that comes from platitudes and clichés. You envision it through the lens of faith, through the promises of God. You envision it beyond your own sight, beyond your own perspective.

It isn't an easy enlightenment to find. When loss is fresh you aren't quite able, not quite ready, but with time, you sit, eyes closed, and you pray to be gifted the understanding of this *better place*.

And eventually you are.

You start seeing things, not *how they aren't* or *how they're not able*, but just as they are—for them. You see that there is a better place, a location more brilliant and worthy than this. You see clearly when you look through their eyes, instead of only your own. You can see a clear and focused view when your pain isn't blinding and heartbreak isn't stealing the light.

Turns out there is a *better place*, though you'll always feel the *best* place was the one when you were together. That truth will never change. That longing will never dissipate.

The **best place** is the one with moments shared, the one with earthly aliveness. The **better place** is the one with flawlessness and glory, the one with heavenly aliveness.

Isn't the whole hope of life to reach heaven, to reach limitless existence?

I'd forgotten the ultimate hope—the hope that we'll all end up in a *better place*, together.

And I no longer despise hearing about the "better place" people speak of because it's heaven. The better place is heaven, which one day will be the only place that matters.

good to see you smile

If they could, they'd whisper, *It's good to see you smile*. They'd tell you that their favorite version of you is the one that smiles effortlessly, without guilt and without hesitation. The kind of smile that you can feel, the kind that you know is authentic—not for a photo opportunity but for the heart.

They'd tell you they love to see you laugh, the kind that makes your whole body wiggle. The kind that makes your eyes water and your breath take a pause. The kind that comes unexpectedly and brings so much joy and bliss it reminds you how incredible it feels, because recently grief has tried to make you forget.

If they could, they'd whisper, *You're making me proud*. They'd tell you that all that you're becoming is so much more profound and purposeful than you can imagine. They'd tell you that while it feels like they aren't there to see it, they've been a part of what's created it. Influence has no boundaries. Love has no limitations.

They'd tell you they love to see you happy because you can still be happy. In fact, it is their only wish for you, to be content and healthy and enjoy each moment of your life, because one day, yours will be completed too.

If they could, they'd whisper, *Thanks for keeping my name alive and my traditions blooming*. They'd tell you that they were never worried about where death would lead but they sometimes worried about being forgotten. That their name would slowly fade from the mouths of those they loved, that their memory would cease to exist.

They'd tell you that every time the photographs get pulled from the cabinet, or each time their name is spoken, they feel loved in ways that only heaven and remembrance can create.

They'd tell you that loving you is easy and effortless—still and always. They'd tell you that they love watching all that you're becoming, even though to you it feels as if they'll never know these newly crafted versions of yourself. They will. They undoubtedly will.

If they could, they'd tell you to use faith as your engine, your fuel. They'd tell you that it's the only thing that sustained them, the only place that gave them hope and promises that wholeheartedly came to fruition. They'd tell you that you have nothing to fear, that the nothingness that haunts you is actually the sacred space in which one day they'll welcome you into forever—limitless forever.

They'd tell you that they know their death felt like a dead end, like a complete stop of your journey. It isn't. It's simply one ending with the opportunity to rebuild and continue in ways that suit you, in ways that inspire and support you—hopefully crafted from their honor and their remembrance.

They'd tell you that earth has expiration dates. Heaven does not. Neither does love. They'd hope you'd let that truth sustain you.

If they could, they'd tell you that they're whispering a million heaven-sent *I love yous*. If you listen, you might hear. It won't sound like their voice, but rather like coincidence. They'd dare you to be open to the beauty that through them, there is no coincidence, only serendipity.

And with time you realize there is no *if they could*. There is only *they are from heaven*.

And they are—from heaven.

So, smile and live and laugh and love—heaven's watching. They're watching.

guard my heart

I tell him to guard my heart—not in a way that lovers do, but in a way that means it will stay, it will keep beating. My mother's heart stopped. She was only fifty-seven. I wonder if maybe I could have guarded her heart so that she'd still be here, so that the cancer wouldn't have stolen her health and ceased her heart from beating.

I tell him to guard my heart—not in a way that husbands do, but in a way that will protect it from being ripped open again by death and loss. I cannot fathom losing someone else. This loss has nearly taken my life too. I don't have to explain these truths, he knows.

I tell him to guard my heart—not in protection built like a fence but more of a force field that allows the good in and the bad deflected. I want my heart to continue knowing love and influence and adoration. I want my heart to forget the impact of death and the way it feels to forever seal the casket of a loved one, making them completely out of reach, completely unalive, untouchable.

I tell him to guard my heart, ensuring it cannot be broken again. The kind of broken that cannot be fixed or healed or mended. The kind that signifies *gone forever*. The kind that placed my name in the obituary of someone incredible, someone I call my mother. I tell him to guard my heart, to protect it from pain and grief, to protect it from harm.

I beg him to please guard my heart.

And I know he would if he could, his watery eyes tell me so. They also tell me that he isn't capable of that type of protection, that kind of safety. He knows I already know those truths. He thinks maybe it's my desperation and my grief that asks, not me.

I think maybe it's both—me and my ache, both of us asking, pleading for a safe haven. Pleading for protection from this loss so that it doesn't duplicate or happen again.

And even through my longing I know this *ask* is too big, this *want* is too much. This man, my soulmate, the love of my life, would do anything for me. And yet, this is beyond his capability, obnoxiously out of his power and control.

And here I am, still, asking hopelessly, for him to please guard my heart.

And I know that he will, to the best of his ability.

And with one simple sentence he does.

I watch as he looks up in intentional and wholehearted prayer and says, "Lord, please guard her heart."

And he will.

They both will.

Each within their capacity—one finite, one infinite.

And I weep and think, *Thank you for guarding my heart—both of you.*

loves me

He loves me like you always prayed someone would, like you always *knew* someone would. I wish you were here to witness it firsthand.

You used to watch me dream of romance, now I live it. You used to watch as I'd get lost in Hallmark movies, now I get lost in his eyes, his embrace, and the life we've so carefully built together—imperfect but beautiful.

Immediately he knew how to love me through it—*through the grief, through the loss, through my fragmented pieces and my raw and harsh vulnerabilities, through waking up each day only to lose you again and again*. Through it all.

He collects my broken pieces each day and dares me to create something with them. And you'd be so proud because I actually do.

He steals my breath with his effortless care and adoration and, even better, finds my breath in times when it has vanished from grief's pain. I never knew the pricelessness, the blessing, of finding a partner that can do both—take your breath away and remind you to breathe.

Sometimes his pride reminds me of yours. He's always proud of me long before I'm ever proud of myself. It's as if you passed that down to him, so that it could stay, so that it wouldn't be gone like you.

You were the first one to show me what selfless, unconditional and authentic love is and was. Now, he reminds me of that love each and every day. Though his love is different from yours, in so many ways they mirror one another. The common thread being me, you both love me.

Love is such a complex thing. It can shatter you and it can save you. I've lived both. I'm living both. But you already know that, of course you do, because as complex as love is, it's also equally transcendent, equally infinite.

You once wrote in your journal—
Love is complete acceptance.
Love is selfless.
Love is unconditional—through good times and bad.

And it's true. And we have that.
Can you see it? I hope you can see it.

if I didn't know better

If I didn't know better, I'd think you were still around. In some ways, it's as if you never left. Your photos still hang in the same spaces as before, even better, more of them now decorate our walls. We still talk about you—you're still so alive in our hearts.

I swear if I didn't know better, I'd think you were still here—alive.

If I didn't know better, and my heart wasn't shattered in the irreparable way grief breaks it, I'd think you were still here. I'm not sure I've ever comprehended your death or your absence. For a while, I ran from that truth. Eventually, I sat with it. Now, each day I carry that reality with me, though sometimes still naive to the fact that your absence is forever, that my life will not hold additional memories with you in them.

If I didn't know better, and your name wasn't carved in stone to remind me, it'd be easy to think you were still here in the traditional way. It still feels like you've managed to show up for me, for us, with delicate reminders of the unwavering love you have for us—still. When I'm lucky, I find you in the clouds or in the cardinal that visits at just the right time. Though, if I were truly lucky, you'd still be here.

If I didn't know better, and we didn't have memory books instead of new memories, we'd all still think you were here. You have grandchildren you never met who say your name daily. They ask about you and consistently mention how they miss you—a woman they've never met, one who never got to hold their tiny bodies or kiss their chunky cheeks. For them, it's as if they don't know better and you're still here—alive.

I swear sometimes I wish I didn't know better. I wish I could wake up, and this would all be some horrible mistake—some awful kind of nightmare that wasn't actually meant for us, or you. I wish cancer didn't exist and that the "good ones" didn't die young. I wish the good ones, the great ones, stayed—because if they did, you'd be here.

I wish I was unmarked by grief and untouched by profound loss. I wish I wasn't the kind of woman the world labeled motherless, nor the kind of woman with a mother in eternity instead of just a phone call away.

I wish I didn't know the sting and scar of a forever absence. I wish I didn't know what it felt like to deliver a eulogy or pick out a casket for the woman who created me—you. I wish I could go back and savor each minute, each second.

I wish I didn't know better. I wish I didn't wake up each day with this debilitating and transformative truth, but I do.

So, for now, I'll hold on to the days where it feels like I don't know better—the days where you feel like you're right beside me, touching my shoulder in a nudge to keep moving. The days where I swear I hear your whisper or see you in a crowded room. The days where I feel you in the gentle breeze or laugh in remembrance of a time we had together. The days where we're together—even if only in a memory.

And maybe that's the miracle of love—it's so powerful, it defies time, transcends loss, and keeps you eternally present, even when you're not. Because even when I know better, in my heart, I still feel you. And maybe, just maybe, that means you never really left.

healing forever

*"Grief provides hurtful reminders of all we've lost.
Love provides hopeful reminders of all we had."*

XOX, Chels

healing begins, then continues

She asks when healing began. I tell her healing happens all the time. It happens again and again. It happens here and there, both today and yesterday, and further still, too far to be accurately measured. Even more, it will continue, for there is healing that hasn't begun yet. It will rise and stretch when the time is right, in places you haven't even stepped yet—when your heart is ready and your head has acknowledged the hard truths that cannot be undone.

Healing isn't a finite task. It is an infinite one—one that is never fully accomplished or completed. Instead, it's one that *changes with you*, then ultimately uses its influence to *change you*—better equipped to carry heaviness, while still able to internalize exuberance.

The question of when it begins is irrelevant because whether it comes immediately or a lengthy time down the road, when it does arrive you must work at it, recognize it, and appreciate it so that it will stay—so that it will continue indefinitely. For the goal is constant healing—healing into each tomorrow, perpetually.

She asks if healing can happen for everyone, including her. The answer is a sincere yes. Healing is not limited in quantity or repetition, though it is a privilege. While everyone receives the opportunity for healing, it cannot be acquired without an individual pursuit to restore our hearts and replenish our souls. It is a choice, even though it sometimes feels like a freedom given to only a select few—the lucky ones.

No matter when healing begins or how long it has journeyed with us, it won't make us whole again, but rather it will aid us in recognizing our longing and allowing it to coexist with joy. Healing is a freedom to carry forward while holding all of the truths of our past and being open to our future—regardless of what it is void of or, even sometimes, what it contains without our approval.

The beautiful truth is that if you want healing and you work intentionally toward healing, it will find you. It will find the hardened pieces of you, and it will soften them. It will take your sharpest edges and taper them with love and grace. It will hold you again and again and again, if you let it. Let it.

It will allow you the opportunity to hold more reminiscence than longing for what cannot be. It will not take away the ache of losing someone but rather remind you that while a body is absent, a relationship, love, and influence still exist. They always will. Can you accept that truth?

Healing is yours, if you want it.

It will not be easy. It will reopen wounds that you bandaged with temporary and precarious things, for to heal, they must be mended with both vulnerability and truth. When you're running from reality, you confuse healing with numbness. Only one is beneficial, and it isn't desensitizing—even though that's the easiest approach most times. To feel hope and happiness and radiance, you must also feel and comprehend their contradictions, as harsh as that is.

Healing cannot be forced or wished into existence. It is work, both soul work and heart work among many other types. It is a solitary job, no matter how many resources, friends, or therapists are around to assist. It's a process of protection, shifted into a transformation of enduring freedom and acknowledgment—forever changed by both the loss and the love.

Healing is possible and it begins again and again and again forever if you let it.

Let it.

shape my future

Am I going to let my mother's death shape my future—or her life and her love? That is the question I ask myself each morning, knowing that I have the choice, each and every day, to choose pain as either my motivator or my excuse. To let grief be my reasoning and purpose or to let it be her. Let it be all that she wanted for me and all that she hoped I'd accomplish.

I have to actively and boldly choose her life and her love and her influence each day. I have to choose living over the powerful heartbreak and agony of her absence and, more importantly, over simply surviving. We haven't been given added time just to survive—our loved ones would want us to flourish. Their goals and their hopes for us didn't change with their entrance into eternity. So, each day we have to remind ourselves of that task—the one that encourages us to not just be in this world but also belong and appreciate the gift of continued living.

This doesn't mean grief and loss are easy. Healing is a constant pursuit. It cannot be won or fully achieved on this side of heaven. Which means the reality is that sometimes grief is there when I wake up like a weight on my heart that says, *Not today*. Like an ache deep in my soul that says, *Don't forget me. I'm here too. I'm always here.*

On those days, I listen because usually one of grief's lessons or wisdom or healing comes from the reminders of ache and longing and absence. The truth is that grief comes and stays with every breath and every beat of your heart, but with time you learn that it's not there to take your life too. It's not there to debilitate you with pain. It's there to empower you with the knowledge of life's fragility so that you'll appreciate it more. It's there to have you embrace your future, instead of running from it. It's there to give you the perspective of what death is and what it isn't. It's there to say, *I don't want you to forget the pain because I want you to honor and cherish the love you were given, which cannot and will not ever leave.*

It's there to teach you things only grief can—even when you're not ready and not willing. It's there to make the choice of living beautifully more complicated but not impossible.

Now, years after my mother's death, I'm ready most days to courageously proclaim and choose that her life and her love will be what shape my day and my future. I breathe in all the love that she filled me with each day that she was here, and breathe out the reminders of her death and the trauma from her final moments. I remember her the way she'd want me to—the version of her that made me laugh, that made me feel deeply cared for, and that championed better things for me than I ever dreamed or believed possible.

The choice is easy when I realize I'm choosing what she'd want for me over what my pain tells me I'm capable of. We're so much stronger than we give ourselves credit for. She used to remind me of that. Chances are, your person did too. So, each day when I wake up and suffering and torment give me a thousand reasons to be angry or sad or even worse—paused and stuck—I choose her.

I choose her life and her love to shape my future, and I hope you'll do the same. Even when it's not easy, and especially when it's hard—choose them to shape your future. It's much more magnificent and meaningful that way.

nothing else to do

The casket is closed, another defining moment of finality, another profound moment of witnessing the sacred culmination of a life. You give it a final touch and gently speak the last words that give your breath the only remaining opportunity to be tucked with them forever.

When there is nothing else you can do—**you say goodbye**.

You open photo albums. You immerse yourself in the memory. You close your eyes and try to remember exactly what it felt like to be there, with them. You replay it like a movie, searching for the sounds, the smells, the experiences. It's not the same joy and exhilaration as it was back then, but for a brief moment, you feel alive again in ways that you only knew when they were alive too.

When there is nothing else to do—**you remember**.

You've finally stopped running from the pain, but in all of the years of grief's solo marathon you've never been able to succeed, to reach a finish line—pain and longing outlast you every single time. To remedy the consequences and emotions created by the death of a loved one, you realize you must sit with harsh truths and work diligently to remain hopeful and steady in your pursuit of living a fulfilling life.

When you're ready, there is only one thing you can do—**you heal**.

After the goodbye, which isn't actually *good* at all, and after the remembering and after the continuous healing, you remain in a cycle of goodbyes and remembering and healing. You remain changed and constantly changing. You also remain loved—permanently, no matter the circumstance.

After death finds someone you love and grief finds you, there is simply nothing else to do but remember and heal, heal and remember—forever.

When you're ready, with love and hope and grief and remembrance, there is one thing you must do—**you live**.

First you say goodbye. Then, you remember. Eventually, you heal. And finally, you live.

can you heal?

Can you heal without using other people—without defining heroes and solutions other than yourself? Can you heal without using busyness to propel you? Can you heal without the attempt to fill the holes of grief and mourning with material things that won't fix or fit those vacancies?

Can you heal, alone?

Can you make the effort right now to heal in ways that have benefit and purpose? Can you work, not to distract yourself from the pain but to learn from it, to grow from it? Can you boldly and bravely choose to keep stepping into the future, even though you're scared and tired and in constant fear of both the past and the present?

Can you heal if you don't truly understand what healing is?

Healing is a challenge you must meet each day—a project that is never fully completed.

It's acknowledging that numbness isn't an answer but rather a false sense of escape. It's reminding yourself of that truth again and again until you believe it.

Healing isn't a journey to becoming whole again. It's sitting with reality and your emotions over and over until your heart understands that you will never be fully whole again, at least not in the ways you envision. Healing is recognizing that the profound beauty of those empty spaces comes from accepting that they are forever saved for the people whose absence created them.

Can you heal in a way that suits you, in a way that saves you?

Can you accept that healing isn't about never feeling the pain of loss again? Pain and heartbreak will remain inevitable. Healing isn't a shield from suffering. It's the guide that allows you to be better equipped and prepared for the next time it comes. It's the relentless quest to overcome suffering each time it visits.

Are you ready to heal?

Healing is a choice. It's an intentional decision to keep stepping, keep trying, keep breathing even when you can't see beyond the next step, the next movement. It's the toughest pursuit you will endure.

It's demanding.
It's relentless.
It takes courage and grit.

Healing isn't just sitting with the ache and longing, it's wrapping it in love and grace and compassion, knowing it will feel more like a curse at the beginning than a rescue. Eventually, with time, resiliency, and gained perspective, healing will become the force instead of the pain.

Are you ready to heal? Do you even want to? It starts with wanting to.

I hope you heal, and then I hope you never stop.
You can heal.

she is you

She's exhausted but she is working each day to lighten grief's load.

She holds healing like a badge of honor and hides her sorrow as much as she can. She's learned the places her heart is safe and the places that are harmful. She wonders if that should be people instead of places.

Safe people. Harmful people.

Those who see her for who she is hiding and not for the character she so often plays. She thinks healing and authenticity will both come with time.

Grief stole who she was. Now, she's not sure where or what the real version of her is, or if she's supposed to create it.

She cries often, but usually when no one is around. She smiles so consistently that people think it's real, that it's genuine. She feels like a fraud, like a fake, at most times and most moments. She doesn't want to.

She carries a weight that sometimes suffocates her, and other times inspires her to keep going. Grief is one of those bruises, those wounds, that almost feels good when you touch it. It solidifies that all of it is real. The pain reminds her that they existed, they lived. It reminds her that the love was genuine, that it was real, for she can feel its absence in her soul.

She's been told it won't always be this way, and she knows that to be true. She can only pretend for so long. Eventually she will have no choice but to heal, to take off the mask and share her hurt and her vulnerabilities with the world. She wonders when she does if it will encourage others to do the same.

She wishes that others had done the same for her, that they had opened the door for the consequences of mourning so she wouldn't have been surprised by them.

She knows healing will not come easy. This isn't her first attempt. She's tried to heal from this death a dozen times, always unsuccessfully. Though if she's honest, her attempts held little effort and usually involved unhealthy and faulty solutions.

She will heal, she's sure of it. Just as she's sure that she will hold this emptiness forever too. Some spaces are reserved for only one person, and when they die, it remains theirs, even though to others it looks like an opportunity, an open seat.

There are no open seats in grief. They remain filled with influence and love, with or without a body draped inside them. She knows that empty seats are a myth, at least to her.

She has been called a legacy and tomorrow she hopes to start becoming one. She doesn't want that priceless truth to get lost in chaos. Today is heavy. She lets it be heavy. Tomorrow will be lighter, or so she prays.

She is exhausted but she perseveres each day to lighten grief's load.

She honors *both* always—ache and remembrance.

She persists.

She stops pretending.

She exists authentically.

She heals.

And she is you.

the rooms that grief built

I picture grief as an escape room, a circus fun house, full of rooms of chaos and transformation instead of fun. Each room leads to another. There are no exits, only transfers—another room, another space of grief and loss to encounter.

Each room has its own challenges, its own lessons. Each room has its own intricacies and cares. You don't win or overcome to get to the next room, the next place. You absorb the meaning and move on—move forward, for you are never allowed the opportunity to go back. You've tried. Those doors, those possibilities, do not exist.

The first room doesn't feel like a room at all. It feels like a haunted house. You're scared of everything, and you swear nothing is real. You stare in disbelief and in shock. You assume this room is meant for someone else, anyone but you. You don't belong, except the tombstone in front of you is marked with the name of your loved one and the wall holds a screen that is replaying the very death and reality you're trying to avoid. Here you're stuck with it, all of it, as if it's the only thing you know, the only moment you remember.

This first room is filled with chaos and destruction. You pick things up and break them, things you'd never do in real life. You wonder if there is such a thing as real life—after all, life has been shortened and ended prematurely for someone you loved.

You enter the next room without knowing how. You blink and instead of horror and death, instead of anger and disbelief, you are in a room that could only be called one thing—numb.

You feel nothing. You move through the steps, either pretending or out of the new responsibility that seems to have called you its master. You make choices and prepare for things like a funeral and a eulogy. And yet, even still, you feel as numb as you would lying on an operating table, subdued and unconscious.

In this room you cannot feel. It's much better than those before it, which is how you know you won't be given the privilege of staying here. While you're numb, feeling nothing, you can also tell that this room is a facade. It's an illusion. And just as you comprehend the mistruths of numbness, you are pulled to the next room.

The next room is dark and somber. It is despair. It is sorrow. In the middle, there is a hole, a trench so deep you cannot see where it leads. As you remember the pain of grief again, as you feel it, you jump—into the hole as if you're Alice in Wonderland. Only you aren't Alice, and this is no wonderland. You had no choice but to jump, this hole was calling your name.

When you reach the bottom, you let the new atmosphere encapsulate you. You let the sorrow spill out. You let everything that was numbed in the previous room come to the surface and seep from your eyes. It feels like you're crying acid. You wonder if you are. It hurts, but in this room, this reality, what doesn't? You stay in this room, this pit, for an undisclosed time—could be a month, could be a year. You're unsure. The only thing you are confident of is that it took help and energy to get you to the next room.

When you get there, you're standing in front of a mirror. You no longer recognize yourself. You read in the fine print of this place that this is common. You noticed it read "common" because "normal" doesn't seem to exist anymore.

The next room is lighter. You wonder if its name might be reminiscence. It feels like a gift. It's a room you're immediately grateful for, which again reminds you that there will be another one after this. You breathe deep and realize it's the first breath that wasn't forced, wasn't searched for.

You scan through old photo albums. You stroll down memory lane. You smile, looking at them in the only way you can now—on paper or on a screen. You are reminded of what it felt like to be loved by them. You feel that love now. You feel honored that they were yours, and you theirs. Honored that most of the beauty, if not all, that you hold was created by them.

You love this feeling. You adore this room. You'll learn with time and after cycles through grief's maze, grief's rooms, that this one is your favorite. The other rooms you enter and cycle through hold complex things like shame, regret, jealousy, and ache. There are also others called hope and faith and gratitude.

You learn that you visit but never get to stay. With time you get better acquainted and familiar with each room. You always leave with an "I'll see you later," for you know you'll visit again, either placed there by grief's fickle ways or visited by choice and careful selection.

As you live and as you grieve, you are housed in grief's maze, grief's wheelhouse.

Which room are you visiting the most? I hope it is the one called "Living Again," but if not, at least the one called "Healing."

only you

Some days there is no inspiration, there is only you.

Some days there is no visible hope and no strength to be seen or found.

There is only you.

Some days you'll want answers for unanswerable questions and miracles for prayers that have already expired—and there will only be you.

Some days there isn't a thing or a person to pull you out of despair, there is you—only you.

But you are the one for this job. The only one, in fact.

You will be the answer. You will be the prayer. You will be the intention.

You will be the continuation of things they started and can no longer do.

You will be the extension, the follow-through, only you.

There is only you.

Only you can heal from this heartbreak and recover from this grief.

Only you can find beauty in tomorrow and the desire for all the ones that follow.

Only you can place remembrance above regret and legacy above lament.

Only you can execute and accomplish this task, this responsibility.
You are all that you need.
Enough. Worthy. The one.

You are the hope. You are the strength. You are the purpose, *your* purpose.

You are the evolution, both of them and also of you, with new perspective and new awareness, with a new identity built from everything, not only the things laced with sorrow.

You are the only one.
And you are here.
And here is enough because here means surviving.
Here means still having opportunities and breaths and tomorrows.
Here means the chance to live, and most importantly, to heal.
Here means alive.

You are alive.

You are alive.
You are alive.
You are alive.
Remember it. Believe it. Act on it.
Choose it.

You are here. You are alive. And only you can be the one to do something with it—something meaningful, something worthwhile, something with a purpose that says, *I can do this. I will do this. Me and only me.*

And it will be true. You will.
You, only you.

feel like

I feel like I need to heal but also like I need to lose thirty pounds.

I feel like I need to enjoy life but also like I need to focus on the growing list of to-dos in front of me.

I feel like I need to be a better mother and wife but also like I need to be a better daughter and friend—just better, at everything.

I feel like at any given moment I should be doing two things, three things even, maximizing my time. So, I do, and then I feel as though I'm giving 20 percent to all things, which realistically means failing at all things.

I feel like I've been handed a chore list with someone else's name.

I feel like I have to hold a legacy and also create one when I can barely hold the weight of grief or create anything other than my next breath.

I feel like I need to pretend for others and smile even when it's unnatural and a complete betrayal to everything felt in my heart and soul.

I feel like I need to speak the names of those I've lost but not in a way that makes others uncomfortable or intimidated.

I feel like I have to show others that grief is okay while constantly being shown that it's not.

I feel like I have to do things and be things—other than myself, other than broken.

I feel like time is slipping away at a pace that I cannot keep up with, because it is slipping away at a pace that I cannot keep up with.

I feel like my heart remembers hope, but I've forgotten.
I want to remember. I want hope.

I feel like something inside of me believes in healing, in life after profound loss, and I want to believe it too—that survival is possible, even when being whole again might not be.

I feel like I'm not okay but also like I'm not giving up.
And that's enough for now.
I feel like that's enough for now.

stepping beyond

There is only one life you can save. It was never theirs. It is yours.

You have the unique ability, the uninvited calling, to save your life from being swallowed whole by grief and the expectations of others.

You must choose, actively choose, to start living—
beyond the pain.
beyond the ache.
beyond the sorrow.
beyond the unknowns.

Beyond it all—knowing that it doesn't mean forgetting or diminishing all that's happened, all that's been lost.

Beyond it all—to each tomorrow, because for now you've been handed tomorrows.

You must rise from this heartbreak, not because it is easy or simple but because you are called to—both by those who love you here and by those who love you from heaven.

You can survive this grief.

It won't be in a way that erases *what is* or comforts *what will never be*, but it will be in a way that allows you to absorb grief like the sun's rays when you're lying on a beach. You feel the warmth, knowing it will change you. It will both darken you *and* make you glow.

Healing is not only possible, it's probable. Grief and pain will try to teach you otherwise. Don't listen.

It happens in little steps of—
remembrance
and patience
and grace
and hope
and faith
and time
and you.

You will survive this—one day at a time and with each step into the beyond, your beyond.

strength

Strength isn't about holding back tears or hiding emotion that seeps from every pore of your body. Strength is about authenticity. It's about vulnerability. It's about carrying memories while simultaneously carrying grief.

It's about remembering, even when it hurts and even when it makes others uncomfortable. It's about knowing boundaries and using them. It's about having the courage to say "no" or "not right now."

It's about visiting graves when you're ready and not when others think you should.

It's about accepting an inherited legacy and one day making something with it.

It's showing the world that grief is normal and okay and not contagious.

It's not lifting weights but lifting yourself off the floor of despair and sorrow.

Strength is living again after loss left you stuck and immobile.
It's carrying forward, not moving on.

It's healing
and healing
and healing.

It's you finding your way in unfamiliar territory, uncharted waters.

It's you honoring a life while still living a life.

Strength is you, in tiny bits and pieces, living and breathing and staying.

Strength is the capability to endure.
And you have endured.

Strength is not forgetting.
And you'll *never* forget.

Strength is you.

memories

"I will forever cling to the pieces of the past.
You're in them."

xox, Chels

when you think of me

When you think of me, how do you feel and what do you see? I fear my memory has become attached to my death in ways that are so entangled you cannot see that the two are not the same. The two are so very, very different.

My life should be my memory. My love should be my legacy. My death should be but the tiniest blip in the story. It should be only the smallest piece of the memories I built, the memories we built—together.

Before I died, I lived. That is the truth I want you to ground yourself upon. That is the foundation of remembrance that I want you to cherish and honor. I do not want the harshness of my death to overshadow the beauty of my life.

My life was created and shaped by decades of living, years and years of experiences and relationships. My death was the opposite. It was quick, gone in an instant, with no effort and no help. I wish your mind would have forgotten it just as quickly. I wish I could shape your thoughts with only life—meaningful and purposeful life, both mine and yours.

I know you keep the heartbreak of my finality tucked inside like both a nightmare and a badge of honor. I wish I could steal that piece of you, that memory, that chaos. I'd replace it with the beauty and authenticity of each day I was gifted, each day we were gifted together.

My death left me forever changed, bodiless and different. It did not make me "gone." Grief tries to tell you differently—stop listening. Listen to me. Listen to my voice from the past. Listen to the lessons I worked so hard to teach you. Do you remember the biggest and boldest one? It was love—always love.

Listen to love now that you can't truly listen to me.

When you think of me, think love not death. Think of all the days before the one etched on my headstone. Think of my life with more intentionality and focus than you do my death. You grieve my passing so effortlessly, can you celebrate my life with that same competence, that same robustness?

When you think of me, how do you feel and what do you see?

I hope you let my life be my memory. I hope you let my love be my remembrance. I hope you allow yourself to become my legacy—built from life's celebrations, not death's mourning.

My life was my defining factor, my influence and my success. Think of me, not as someone lost or gone or dead but as someone unforgettable who lived.

Think of me, always, through life, not loss.

Remember me that way.

following

Death used to be the thing that followed me—her death. It clung to my memories as if it was the only one. It haunted me with the final moments. It taunted me with the list of regrets from my heart's "should haves" and "wish I would haves." It was relentless and harsh.

And it followed me—everywhere, into each new day and each new experience.

I woke up to be reminded that she wasn't coming back. Her absence followed me. There was a constant void where she had always been, where I always wanted her to be. There seemed to be both a shadow of darkness and a bottomless abyss beside me at all times. One simply stole the light, the other was a pit of pain so deep I assumed it could never be emerged from.

Her absence followed me—everywhere.

Her memory became clouded by the visions of the end, her end. After seeing her lifeless body in a wooden box, a chosen tomb, grief designed how she appeared in my mind. She became reduced to her final minutes—yellowed skin, emaciated face and body, wrinkles that seemed to appear in days instead of years. This version of her had replaced all the others. It displaced her smile, her beauty, and most of all the health she had, until the moment she didn't.

Her death and the image of it followed me.

I was accompanied, not by the past but by one singular moment of it. I did not want to be chased or pursued. I wanted to be as alone as I felt. I wanted to have privacy from grief's undoing and death's consequences and transformations.

I did not want her death to follow me. I wanted her life to follow me. I want her legacy and her guidance and her love to be the embedded memory, the lasting image. She would want the same.

Her death was reality. The grief of her loss is real. Those images of her were etched from cruel, authentic experience. And while I can hold the truth of these statements, these actualities, I do not have to be infested by them. I do not have to be followed by them like a character in a suspense film. Her life wasn't scary, so her memory shouldn't be either.

The past is real. It cannot be changed. But not all pieces are meant to be replayed in our brains like a cycle of punishment, a chosen self-harm. Our memories should be built from greatness and goodness. We should be followed by the snapshots of laughs and traditions and times that we wish we could preserve forever, not the times we wish we could escape.

I'm no longer followed by her death, though grief still walks beside me. I'm followed by her honor and her remembrance, the visions of her she'd pray we'd preserve, the ones she would have chosen for us. I'm followed by her faith in eternal healing and transformations I haven't been close enough to observe. I'm followed by her blind trust and her unwavering hope. I'm followed by her smile and her beauty. I'm followed by her at her best.

Her death will no longer follow me. Her love and legacy will.

Can you say the same?

she stays in the before

I see her in the back of my mind, the woman I used to be before I became heartbroken by grief. I see her smile without guilt and laugh without hesitation. I see her freedom and her blissful naivety. I see her mindfulness, the way she can soak up the present moment without feeling tethered to life's fragility, and how endings can happen at any time, especially when you're not prepared for them. I see a life that hasn't been touched by death yet, one that holds only little ripples of ache from mundane disappointments, not catastrophic casualties.

I don't need a photo to be reminded of that person, though she feels more like a stranger than an extension of who I once was. I can close my eyes and replay the way I walked without the weight of a forever goodbye. I can see the way my body flowed without burden or fear, even though I don't remember what that felt like. I can see the way my eyes glistened with radiance instead of glossiness from a constant search for someone no longer there.

I can see a person who doesn't know endings or the way time escapes so quickly. I can see a person who wears colorful clothes from boutiques instead of a thick cloak of grief from burying our mother. I see a woman who has a mother, not the memory of one.

I wish I could ask her to tell me about her version of our mother, the one that is still alive. I want to remember her the way I used to, the way that was only a phone call away, not a trip to the cemetery. I wonder which version would be my mother's favorite, the old me or the new one. I wonder if the answer would break my heart.

Both the woman I can picture, the one from the past, and the woman I am today hold gratitude and limitless love for our mother. Our mother would be proud of that, though it wouldn't surprise her. We both make our love known, one in life and one in death.

I wonder if you placed us side by side if she'd find beauty and worth in me, the way I can so easily in her. Would my missing pieces be detected, even though they are invisible? Would she immediately recognize the way she is me and I am her? Or have we become such an inversion, such drastic contradictions, that we mimic strangers more than being a mirror of what was and what is?

I can see her, but she has no concept of me, nor a concept of all of the surprises of what life will look like—both the blessings that we were granted and the things that haunt our minds and our future. I'm glad only one of us can feel the consequences of grief and the way death creates more casualties than the person who has been eulogized. I'm glad only one of us is exhausted by a constant pursuit to heal. I'm glad only one of us is impacted by the responsibility of replicating traditions and executing legacies.

She gets to stay in the before and I in the after. Only one of us must bear the burden of loss and it is me. I get to know her as a memory in the same way that I know my mother as a memory—both people gone, one by death and one by unexpected and involuntary transformations.

The hope is that one day when an even further version of me looks back on who I am right now, she'll be proud, knowing that instead of allowing resilience and strength to be clichés, I embodied them. She'll recognize that I fought for healing in the same way I fought to keep my mother's name alive.

For now, I reflect, encapsulating an earlier version of me, the one before grief. She's so beautiful and free. She gets to stay in the before, with my mom, and there is no place I'd rather her be.

She gets the beauty of before, and I get the beauty of remembering, remembering what was once me.

standby

She's gone but her memory is telling me to stop living like I'm on death row, to stop living like I'm caged without a future beyond the walls of grief. It's as if she can see me from heaven, only to find I'm confined by the heartbreak of grief, no longer utilizing my breath and my lungs for the potential they have, which is my life.

Their potential is my life—a life that is going unlived and unused. One death, her death, has paused things and destroyed things. It has altered every entity of me. I witnessed her final moments on earth, and then the final responsibilities of her death, and then I placed myself in a confinement of mourning.

I let grief imprison me. I let darkness confine me. I felt alone so I placed myself in solitary confinement, both to ensure no one would have to witness my unraveling and to keep outsiders comfortable in a world they were still happy with—but a world that to me felt suddenly unfamiliar and unloving, harsh and incomplete.

And stuck in this space of ache and longing, this space of loneliness and a decomposition of things that I loved, her memory appeared in my mind, so real I swear it could have been her. It reminded me that I am not a prisoner to grief. I am not a lost soul in the midst of her death. I am not gone—she is, though not as gone as it seems, not as gone as it feels.

I have placed myself in this prison, in this space that mimics death row, failing to realize the resiliency and the aliveness that I still hold so naturally, so purposefully. This death, her death, was not meant to be a blockade or a border for additional life, for additional memories. Instead, she hoped it would be a spotlight that shined on the things that mattered most, the things like time and love. She hoped instead that it would be like a launchpad that catapulted me to the next thing, because for me there are next things.

She knew her death would sting, that it would leave a gaping hole. She didn't realize, nor want, her death to be an excuse to place my life on standby—paused and waiting. There is a substantial difference, I realize, between breathing and living. She's calling me to do both.

She's challenging me, encouraging me, to escape this self-built prison, this personally made confinement, and live—truly live.

Our lives are not given or created to be placed on pause, on standby. They are made to be lived. Lived with all things, all experiences—some of them painful, some of them peaceful.

Her memory finds me in walls of my own making, though I say they're built from grief. Suddenly, I'm ashamed of this house of heartbreak that I've fabricated. Instead of using the tiny stamina I have to construct something meaningful, something she'd be proud of, I've crafted a space of only death and darkness and despair.

Those things exist, they are unavoidable in both life and grief, but they are not the things intended to hold the power or the creation, and certainly not the influence, to live by and live in.

Her memory found me in a cage of heartbreak and grief, a holding cell that had no door and no lock, though I always envisioned one. Her memory pulled me up from the ground, held my hand and walked me out into the light—into the life that was still there, patiently waiting for me.

And now, I live, not just breathe or exist.

I live because her memory and her influence and her love reminded me I was made for more than standby. I was made, not to be imprisoned by grief but to live a life beyond my biggest heartbreak and my most profound losses.

I live because her memory is worth keeping alive and my life is worth living until I become only a memory too.

Her memory found me and reminded me to live—and I do.

hearing your name

The first time someone spoke your name after you died it sent a tidal wave of grief through my heart. It scorched my soul with grief's pain when they asked how you were.

Dead—you were dead.

But I couldn't speak the truth. That simple four-letter word stung with a harshness I did not want attached to you—not your life or your death. I stood there speechless. He repeated the question, not knowing it wasn't my ears that had given out—it was my speech, my tongue, my mind.

And still the answer remained the same, so I was forced to answer as best as I could.

He did what people always do, apologize for an outcome they didn't create, a death they had nothing to do with. We both parted ways—him relieved, I'm sure. Me—broken.

The next time someone spoke your name, I smiled. I hadn't heard it from someone other than family in months. It felt like a treat, the kind you get for doing something special. I wondered if the "something special" was simply surviving this loss, this ache.

They told a story of you, saying your name again and again until I eventually lost count. You were talked about so effortlessly, your name said with such frequency, an outsider would have thought the memory was from last night, not last year. They would have assumed you were still here—more than a name, more alive than only a memory.

What a powerful thing a name can be when speaking it has the ability to bring you back, if only for a brief glimmer of reminiscence and reflection. Each time your name is spoken it makes you feel, it makes you seem, alive—so, so, alive.

Your name said aloud is you being remembered aloud.

I want you to be remembered out loud, affectionately and with pride. I want everyone to hear your name so often, so vibrantly and wholeheartedly, that they think they know you too, even if they don't, even if they didn't.

And I realize how far I've come.

In fresh grief, your name used to leave me breathless with longing and mourning, a reminder of your fate, your absence. Now, your name is a link to your presence, a reminder of the love and influence you left behind. Giving us a chance to tell your stories, a chance to keep you alive—and we do, each time we say your name.

speaking of her

"You talk like she is living," he says. I feel pride until he continues, "You remember she is not?"

Of course I remember my mother is dead, gone. How naive of him to think that one second of a day goes by without comprehending and remembering that truth.

I talk like she is living because she once lived.

I talk like she is living because it keeps her alive in ways only the mourning can appreciate and experience, in ways only grieving hearts can grasp and understand.

He knows I live with the truth of loss and grief. He fails to see how the mention of a dead person's name stirs anxiety and a discomfort that he hasn't claimed yet, though it is his.

He doesn't wonder if my mind is altering a truth, a reality. He wonders if grief can steal your mind the way death steals people.

Stories of the deceased can make people feel unsettled when they fear waking up ghosts. Ghosts of the living, not the gone.

I talk like she is living, only exchanging the *is* for *was*. A clear distinction that has been overlooked by him though never by me. When you have to replace *is* with *was*, you assume the aliveness of the person was replaced just the same.

Maybe he didn't listen. Maybe he didn't hear it. Maybe he didn't want to hear it.

Or maybe I accidentally spoke in the present tense, said ***is***, because she still

is my mother.
is loved.
is missed.
is important.
is remembered.
is ____ (fill in the blank of a million incredible things).

I speak about her as if she is living because I still want her to be. And I'll always choose speaking of her with aliveness, ensuring her memory and influence remain alive in me.

I will speak of her, always, with vitality.

And one day, when death touches someone he loves, and grief touches him, he'll do the same. And I'll let him.

And we'll both speak like they are living—living though only in a memory, only in their legacies, living.

visited

She says the names of the gone, the deceased, so they will notice what is missing. She wants no one to forget. If they forget, her loved ones die again, this time forever. Lost and gone forever.

Lost from memory.
Lost from impact.
Lost from influence.
Lost.

She thinks of all the graves that no one visits anymore. She thinks about how their names have been forgotten, even worse—their lives. She fears that kind of finality for her loved ones, for her, for everyone.

She says their names out loud. She shares their stories out loud so people know they existed. To keep them in existence, if only in ways that are felt instead of seen. Ways that remain real and important.

If the world can see and remember and acknowledge what is missing, who is missing, then they'll acknowledge what once was—them. They once were.

A memory is only as good, as impactful, as its longevity.

A legacy is only as infinite and meaningful as its memory, its impact.

To ensure both are lasting she must remind people. She must introduce the names and influence to those who never witnessed them personally. She must both nudge remembrance and make new introductions.

Grievers don't say the names of the dead for attention.

They don't say them for sympathy, nor for pity.

They say them to ensure a name is remembered, a life and legacy are honored, and for the hope that no grave, no final resting place, ever goes unvisited.

The goal is that we all remain, visited—forever.

peekaboo

I sit at your grave waiting to hear "Peekaboo!" and to see that suddenly you're back. You always came back.

Hands up. Face covered. Gone.
Then, *Peekaboo*.
And back, always back.

As a kid when we played peekaboo, you taught me that people go away but they always come back.

And yet, here I am, at your grave. And you haven't come back.

You're gone, so very gone.

Peekaboo. Peekaboo. Peekaboo.

I feel only the *boo* of those words, only disappointment.

Why do we teach children that people always come back—if they don't.

I can make a list of people who never came back:

You, invaded and plagued with cancer—no peekaboo, no coming back.

My cousin's grandmother, Alzheimer's, a mind gone—no coming back.

My friend, lost to drugs and addiction—no coming back.

A cemetery, this cemetery, filled with death. Bodies buried, lives buried—no coming back.

Peekaboo. Peekaboo. Peekaboo.

A game we play in youth that solidifies a truth that time turns to a fallacy.

People don't always come back.
People don't always survive.
Life isn't a game of peekaboo.

Life is an adult version of hide-and-seek, always searching, only to find that things are hidden so well, they're unreachable.

A game taught us that people disappear temporarily. Life teaches us that eventually absences are permanent—especially the ones that lead to heaven.

In youth, a simple and quick game promised presence. In adulthood, life teaches absence—death's absence, forever and harsh.

And I sit at your grave, that same child though fully grown, waiting to hear you say,

"Here I am. Here I am. Peekaboo."

a gift—remembered

He walks in holding a small red bag. The package is opened to reveal a tiny and delicate keepsake. He smiles and says, "It was my mother's."

His mother has been gone for decades. To some she might even be forgotten—not by him, never by him.

This breathtaking gift is evidence of a legacy, of an unforgettable influence. He handed down a piece of her and suddenly she is alive again.

Her name is being spoken.

People who never knew her are asking for stories, for pictures.

She has risen from the ashes of time's impact on loss and memory. She has risen to be recollected and reminisced again.

Her legacy is awake and thriving in a place some stand never knowing it existed, until now, in this moment. She's meeting people for the first time through those who love her, through him.

Once everyone is gone, we find a perfect place to keep this gifted piece of inheritance.

We want it visible.

We want to keep her visible.

Now, her memory will live here with us too.

He walked in with a gift and left with an additional space to keep his mother's memory and legacy alive.

And now it sits on a shelf and in our hearts right next to the memories and love and legacies of our own mothers.

Legacies united.
Influence revived.
Lives remembered.
Again.
Always.

I see you all the time

She stares at the picture, a moment frozen in time—joy, love, and life radiate from the photo. She is mesmerized by the beauty of her mother. Her smile is so familiar, it's as if she saw it yesterday. She did not. Her mother has been gone for years; the exact number is always too harsh for her to speak aloud. Her eyes fill with tears, sometimes from gratitude and sometimes from grief, as they always do when the memories flood in.

She delicately touches the picture and whispers, "I see you all the time, still. I see you in the goodness of others. I see you in every person that loves you. I see you in the purple butterflies and the vibrant red cardinals. I still see you, all the time—not physically here, but in hope and in reminiscence."

Her mother glances down from the sacred spaces of eternity. She'd recognize those compassionate blue eyes and that dramatically slouched stance anywhere—her daughter. Even from the gloriousness of heaven she sees her, and even more profound, she loves her from there too.

She looks beyond perpetuity and thinks, *I see you all the time, still. I see you in your happiness, and also in your ache. I see you with more truth and authenticity than you even see yourself. I see you struggle and I see you succeed. I wish you knew, that while you still see me, I still see you too.*

They see each other all the time—one from heaven, one from memory.

He stares at the golf clubs tucked into the corner of the garage. He hasn't had the strength to use them yet, they belonged to the greatest man he's ever known—his father. Each time he catches a glimpse of them he's transported back to the memories on that fairway. He's grateful to have them but that doesn't mean that they don't sting.

He pulls the worn and well-loved putter from the bag and says, "I see you in your glory, which was always with these clubs in your hand. I see you all the time, still. I see you in your favorite chair screaming for the blue and white. I see you in the backyard mowing in perfect rows. I still see you all the time and when I'm lucky, I see you in me."

His father peeks down from the blessed spaces of eternity. He'd recognize those clubs and that boy, though grown, from anywhere, even heaven—his son. Even from this far he sees him, and even more profound, he loves him from there too.

He looks through perpetuity and thinks, *I see you all the time, still. I see you in your big moments and more profoundly in your smallest. I see you for all that you are and all that you will be, versions of yourself you haven't even become yet—all loved, all worthy, all you. I wish you knew, that while you still see me, I still see you too.*

They see each other all the time—one from heaven, one from memory.

They see each other beyond eyes and beyond vision. They see one another with heart. One from eternity. One from reminiscence. Both from love.

We tearfully proclaim on earth, "I see you all the time, still."

The others smile from heaven and say, "I see you too."

What beauty it is to be seen—from anywhere.

lessons & strength

"She asks—who is the most profound and influential teacher you've ever had? I reply—grief."

xox, Chels

grief as a teacher

They say grief is a teacher. A source of wisdom and knowledge we're meant to know. But why did someone I love have to die to learn these lessons? Are there not safer ways to deliver these insights? Are there not more delicate ways to imprint these knowings on my mind?

My life has been filled with teachers I've loved and a few who weren't meant for me—the ones a bit too harsh, the ones who erased little pieces of me to be who they needed me to be.

Grief has been one of those teachers.

It drilled and taught and drilled and taught lessons for a class I never signed up for. Sessions that held pain disguised as knowledge. I wish there was a syllabus for this course and that grief would have introduced itself up front. I would have told it this wasn't the right place, the right classroom, for me—not yet. Instead, I was placed here like some kind of punishment, some kind of detention. As if watching someone I love die wasn't penalty enough.

Not only do I have to feel the pain, experience it, but also the world tells me I have to learn from it too. How bold it is to require the mourning to hold both the responsibility of healing and the accountability that it better mean something too.

Who appointed grief anyway? Who hired it for its wisdom and its perspective? Couldn't we have learned the lessons of life's limits and death's destruction in gentler ways? Couldn't it have been part of a lecture, a concept we discussed, a movie wheeled in on one of those carts from back in the '90s? Something we'd learn by observing the idea, not personally experiencing the ache.

Because if I watched grief, if I observed mourning, if I witnessed breath leaving someone and their heartbeat slowing until it no longer beat, I would have felt it even if it wasn't my own. And maybe I would have learned grief's lessons before I was forced. Maybe I would have learned them early enough so their lessons could have an impact now, and not just in the after. I would have had the chance to comprehend the impact of photographs or the pricelessness of quality time with those I love. Maybe I would have known to call more and visit every chance I got. Maybe I would have learned to cherish time because before you can pray for another tomorrow it has already been stolen from you.

They say that grief is a teacher, and it is. But why, instead, are we not teachers of grief, the sharers of its truth, the instructors of its transformative nature and its powerful impact? Why do we wait for grief to come to discuss life's impermanence and love's depth and the art of presence over perfections? Why do we wait until a heart is broken and a life has been transformed to share about resilience and empathy? Why do we wait until someone is covered in darkness to show them how death shifts identities and the nonlinearity of grief and healing?

Why can't we teach grief before last breaths have been taken and bodies have been lowered into the earth? If stories hold power, then why do we hide them until they're no longer stories, but memories?

Are we afraid that teaching grief would mean inviting sorrow, or worse, inviting death to come? Are we worried that resilience and grit would be learned prematurely? Are we worried about normalizing it so that people remain afraid of death and terrified of losing someone they love? Even though everyone dies? Yes, everyone.

We need to learn grief.

To dispel the myths, to discount the incorrect nature of its makeup.

To create a language that feels common and not scary and shameful.

To create a community that is equipped and ready before it is needed. Isn't a proactive approach the best?

Learning grief, knowing it, won't allow the deceased to return.
It won't prevent the ache and the longing.
But it will lessen the surprises, the mistruths, and the unknowns.

If grief has been your teacher, go share its lessons so it won't be too late for someone else. Death is the wound. Pain is the wisdom. Grief is the teacher.

And you can be a teacher too.

avoiding tears

She tries to avoid tears. In fact, she despises them. If something evokes emotion that sends evidence of feelings streaming down her face, she wants to hide. She wants no visibility of her pain or her heartbreak, and certainly not her grief. She thinks that without proof, maybe it can lessen, and if she's really lucky, maybe it can evaporate.

She thinks of crying as a weakness, not as a symbol of life's experiences—both beauty and sorrow—for usually it's the latter that sends her into a tear-filled sentimental episode. Before loss, she can't recall a time she cried—not in frustration or happiness or the in-between. She knew how to control and contain things—until this loss of someone special, someone irreplaceable.

Maybe that's what this is about—control, or lack thereof. Maybe tears are an unavoidable testimony of her grief. A testimony she has no desire to provide confirmation of, for her heart holds that truth daily and it nearly leaves her breathless.

She says that tears are unproductive, for they cannot turn back time or transform her reality. They cannot provide an answer to her *why* or create breaths in places where air can no longer reach. Because of these truths, she spends no time allowing herself the grace to weep, for it cannot be a solution and instead has only left her more exhausted and drained.

She works each day to carry the weight of grief, not realizing that she's adding immeasurable heaviness by harnessing her emotion instead of setting it free.

I can't fault her for that—healing is a complicated quest, one that's never truly complete or finished. I myself have run, though never from tears; those always find me, ready or willing.

Looking at her, I wonder where heartbreak goes if you tuck it down and pretend it doesn't exist. Most things can't grow in darkness and isolation. Heartbreak seems to be an outlier. It grows best when being ignored and left unacknowledged. Pain and grief are the same. Avoidance is their fuel. Denial amplifies their power.

You can certainly shift involuntary tears to forced or managed composure. You cannot, however, erase emotion. You can resist its force, but you cannot eliminate its presence.

Composure is her art, a skill she's mastered to perfection. I wish she knew that tears and emotions aren't an enemy. They are the undeniable receipts for empathy. They are the unapologetic expressions of love. They should be welcomed as a natural release, just like clouds and rain or a breathtaking waterfall.

I wonder who taught her to be ashamed of crying or if it was learned through the absence of tears around her. I wonder when she learned to hide and manipulate the truths of her heart and the realities of her soul. I wonder if she looks at others in sadness and sees meekness and inferiority.

I wish I could push a button and release her of the suppressed sadness and sorrow she holds inside. As someone who holds grief too, even when she thinks she's hidden it well, I know it's there—always there. I wish she'd feel safe enough to free herself from the responsibility of holding back. I wish she knew that tears and crying are okay. I wish she'd have never learned or felt otherwise.

It takes strength to let go and maybe that's what she's afraid of—the letting go. To her, releasing her emotions and tears might feel like letting go of what once was. Maybe she's holding in the tears to keep every single piece of memory and sentiment tucked inside, always with her in ways that her loved one can no longer be. Maybe now she holds it all in because she can, so she does, and she will. It's her way of refusing to give up more than she already has.

For now, she decides what she keeps, and her tears are one of those things.

I hope one day she wears her emotional authenticity just as proudly as she does her favorite T-shirt. I hope one day I look into her eyes and see brilliant color, no longer dull and heavy from caging years of grief and life's experiences.

Tears are a testimony—evidence of love, loss, and a million other things. They are proof that we feel and that we live. They are confirmation of our heart, mind, and soul experiences.

Tears are more than vulnerability. They are love. They are silent prayers. They are signs of unspoken sorrow, happiness, and all the in-between. They are not weakness, they are our heart's language of life's moments, life's happenings.

May she one day feel the freedom to speak in the language of tears and lamenting, and may the world be compassionate when she does.

we don't talk about that

They don't bring her up in conversation anymore. They're afraid to say her name or mention her stories. They fear a simple hint of remembrance will make my grief worse, heavier. I think they are most afraid that it will make my grief visible. Those are two very different things.

You cannot make grief worse by remembering. We love remembering. You make grief harsher, more catastrophic, by forgetting. Our fear is in the forgetting.

We gather and we converse but some things we don't talk about. Like the way it feels to watch breath slip from your loved ones for the last time or the way it shatters your heart to sit with someone as their time of death is called. We don't talk about what it's like to choose a casket or write a eulogy. We don't talk about death.

We meet for drinks and for festivities and we call each other friends—but there are still some things we don't talk about. Like the way it feels to bury a parent or the responsibility that comes in all of the days that follow. We don't talk about what it feels like to be someone's daughter one day and suddenly transformed into the family matriarch the next. We don't talk about what it feels like to always miss someone or what it means to be the beneficiary of life insurance or the executor of an estate. We don't talk about the gift of legacies or the responsibility of them.

There are some things we simply do not talk about.

We plan weekend trips and casual nights in, but there are still certain things we don't talk about. Like the way it feels to hear someone you love has an estimated time of living—a timeframe for life. We don't talk about what it feels like to suddenly fear routine doctors' appointments or how a wave of unrelenting anxiety can come just from entering a hospital. We don't talk about the jealousy that tucks itself deep into our souls when witnessing people who still have what we used to, what we want—not things, but people.

We talk about *nearly* everything but *not* everything.
We talk about breakups but not breakdowns.
We talk about diagnoses but not death.
We talk about melancholy but not mourning.
There are some things we just don't talk about.

But why? Why do we hold back some conversations for an empty room or God? Why do we hide pieces of our story or our experience? Is it for comfortability or denial—is it both? Do others not speak the names of the dead in fear that death will become contagious and touch the lives of people they love? If death is the most shared experience in life, why don't we talk about it?

Why do we pretend that we aren't different versions of ourselves once grief arrives? Is it to keep the invites coming and the friends list strong or is it to keep the ability to fit into the spaces we've always fit before? Are we worried that our rough edges will somehow make us outsiders—same puzzle but now we're the wrong piece?

Grief begins with the elimination of a life, a voice. It shouldn't lead to the elimination of authentic and meaningful conversations too. Silencing grief's influence doesn't eliminate its pain, and it certainly doesn't prevent it from eventually reaching others.

There is healing in the telling, in the sharing, in the sitting with emotions and experiences that are not your own. To honor grief, we must acknowledge it—all of us, both the grievers and the ones close enough to witness grief's sting and transformation.

There are some things we don't talk about.
There are some things we don't talk about, but we should.
There are some things we *haven't* talked about—*but we will.*

some days

Some days you need them more than others—all days you need them. Some days you feel as though they were just here, others as if they've been gone for as long as you can remember. Grief is transformative and tricky like that.

Some days you look around and see them in everything—as if they've just left the room or even, dare I say, are still here. Other days you look around, feeling suffocated by the empty spaces and the dark holes that have found every place they once were, every place they should be.

Some days you look in the mirror and smile as you stare at your reflection, but it's their smile. Other days you see them in the faces of strangers on the street, desperately wishing and wondering what they'd look like if it were actually them, right there in your path—your view.

Some days you wonder why them, most days you wonder why so soon. Other days you find yourself at peace, knowing they're free of pain and void of the ravenous disease that was depleting them from all the things that made them vibrant and grand.

Some days you question God and your faith. Other days you stand strong on the beliefs and hopes that they've solidified in you since you were a child. You find faith and hope can be fickle and limited if you let the darkness take hold. So, you vow not to.

Some days grief is dominant, other days it lies dormant—but always there, always constant in some form or magnitude. Some days you feel as if you cannot make it, as if you will not survive the weight of this grief—the weight of this loss.

You will.

Eventually the "some days" get farther and farther apart. The good days, the lighter days, the days of healing and renewed hope, those shine brighter. Those come quicker—appear more often.

And while everyday life is changed, altered by the absence of someone great, someone wonderful, and every day you wish things were different, you wish they were still here, every day also allows you to carry their love and their legacy.

And eventually, those days are the ones that help you not just survive but also live, truly live, until you can meet again.

And someday you will—meet again.

Some day.

because of them

With spite and disdain, he looked at me and said, "You're only who you are because of your parents." He listed my successes, the ones seen from his eyes, from his perspective: "college, house, career. All because of them."

He wasn't saying it as a compliment. He was saying it to lessen my worth and the value of my accomplishments.

It didn't.

His anger hurt and so did the resentment, but the message didn't. His words only solidified my understanding and gratitude for both my life and my parents.

My life and my success *are* because of my parents. Isn't that the goal?

I was raised with the voices of people who told me I could be anything and do anything. I was born with an unwavering love attached to each and every thing that I did. I was grown from their lived experience and their boldness to give me both roots and wings.

I worked hard. I earned things. I gained meaningful opportunities. I saw both losses and wins. And I did it because of them.

Because of the foundation they built.

Because of the ambition they instilled in me.

Because of their encouragement of both curiosity and independence.

Because of the values they gave me and the dedicated work ethic they lived by.

And more than anything, because they believed in me.

All that I am and all that I will be is because of them—some in small ways and some in priceless ways much too large to measure.

Who we are is a collaboration of us and them, a combination of love and legacy, and if we're lucky that's a beautiful thing.

Years after hearing his words and seeing his face, I find myself visiting my mother differently. Now, I sit on the ground where her body is just beneath me, a place where a stone with her name stands, and I think about his words. He wanted them to break me, to tear me down, and instead they are what carry me on my hardest days.

All that I am and all that I hope to be is built from my mother's love and influence, and that has become one of my greatest compliments.

I hope I see him again one day, so I can look at him and say, "You were right. It was because of them. They didn't give me the degree or the house or the job, but they gave me relentless ambition and a sense of purpose. They gave me hope and they gave me love. And I am who I am because of them—what a blessing."

Not everyone has a parent who shapes them in beautiful and productive ways. I assume he isn't one of them. I assume that's where his contempt lies—not in me, but in what he's missed.

I was one of the lucky ones.

I still am.

Alive or deceased, everything that I am is because of my parents. And I'm okay with that. In fact, it's probably one of my best qualities.

Because of her.

Because of them.

I am.

What a treasure.

she is grief

Grief wakes me in the middle of the night. She tells me her work is almost finished. I tell her I'm confused. I'd heard grief lasts forever, that she lasts forever.

She tells me that what I heard is partially true—she does, in fact, last forever though in different forms and different manifestations. She tells me that she is most known for ache and longing, even better known for heartbreak and sorrow. She tells me she is other things too. She tells me that most people forget what she *becomes* and instead only ruminate on how she *began*, how she *started*.

She tells me she's misunderstood but that she gets it. No one wants her around. She arrives only when someone else has died, when someone beloved has been taken from those who desperately do not want that truth, that fate.

She tells me that she arrives harshly because there is no other way. You cannot prepare for her arrival, though she tells me most of us try. All of us are unsuccessful.

She is fickle and she is constant. She is relentless and she is bold. She is a million negative things. She is grief.

She tells me she is purposeful and intentional things too, and dare she even say beautiful. She tells me people forget that most of all, she is love.

She tells me most of us only look at her as an unwanted and horrific visitor. That's the piece of her she hates. The piece she resents most. The piece that keeps strangers, outsiders, scared of her. The piece that keeps others angry with her, spiteful of her.

She wants to explain that we are confusing her with death. She is not death. She is death's consequence. Death's aftermath. People forget about death. They never forget about grief.

She tells me that her work is important, and it is pure. She tells me that she does everything in love and nothing in revenge, even though the stories of her say otherwise. She tells me her entire purpose is to ensure legacies are extended and lives are never forgotten.

She tells me I'm ready for the next thing, grief's next thing.

And before I can be fearful of the transition that is to come, her name tag fades from grief to reminiscence. And I suddenly understand.

Grief will stay. She will stay. Only now, she's built differently. She's shaped differently. She's lighter and filled with greater hope. She is grief but now she is reminiscence too.

At first when she arrived, she was grief *and* pain, grief *and* longing, grief *and* disbelief, grief *and* despair. Now, she is grief *and* hope, grief *and* remembrance, grief *and* honor.

She has always been grief *and* love—but only now do I see it.

She is grief. Who knew she could be so beautiful?

be aware

Be aware of the people who tell you grief can be healed and death's heartbreak can be reversed. It cannot. The people who inform you otherwise are either naive or misinformed. They probably mean well, though they speak mistruths. Those people don't know the way some holes can never be filled and how some wounds leave us changed forever.

Be cautious of anyone who thinks that loss has a timeline or that you should "be over" the death of someone profound and incredible. You go over mountains and hilltops, not grief. Grief can't be climbed. It cannot be outrun. It's more like a new layer of skin, a version of you that replaces the one before.

Be wary of quotes and toxic positivity that make you feel like your pain doesn't matter or that eventually it will be erased by gratitude and appreciation. There is no quick fix, no magic eraser, including authentic gratefulness for what was. Pain is still pain and loss is still loss.

Be cautious of people who tell you grief is hardest during the first year. It isn't that simple or defined. It isn't that scripted or scheduled. Grief is hard in each year, all with their own intricacies and details that highlight the empty spaces and the unfilled chairs in unique and peculiar ways.

Be aware of false promises of complete healing instead of constant and consistent healing. Grief's healing is work that's never quite finished, a project that always needs additional attention and care.

Be mindful of the darkness that will try to consume the light. Worse still, it will try to persuade you that it isn't there, and even harsher, that it never existed in the first place. Light exists, even when you cannot see it. When you cannot comprehend that truth, envision the way nighttime to you is ironically daytime for someone else. Light exists even when we aren't close enough to see it.

Be bold and brave enough to acknowledge that you can anticipate grief's changes and its chaos, but you cannot predict grief's changes and its chaos. It molds and mutates in new forms and new capacities. Just when you think you've figured it out, that you've cracked the code, a new level is unlocked, a new battle has emerged.

Be aware of grief in all its facets and all its truths—the ones you experience, not the ones you're told about in conversations or the ones you've watched in the movies. Learn grief the way it is for you, not the way that makes the world comfortable and your heartbreak hidden.

And one day, when you're ready—be open.

Open to both heal and grieve forever.

Open to hold traditions and larger responsibility.

Open and inspired to inherit legacies and also create one.

Open to the potential to be grounded in love, not loss, because that will make all the difference—your difference.

Be aware of your grief. Be cautious of the world's view of grief. And more than anything, understand that grief is not love's opposite. Grief is love's proof, love's evidence.

Grief is love—don't let anything teach you or tell you otherwise.

lights out

He stands, waiting for grief to come, not realizing it is already there. Anticipating the death of someone he loves—waiting, watching, as final breaths will soon come. Those moments hold grief too.

Grief isn't only death, though it just might be its boldest creator.

When death finds the life he's so desperately praying for, he will soon feel like the lights have suddenly gone out. As if he is surrounded by such intense and powerful darkness he wonders if anything in the room still exists, if he still exists. The only proof of life he knows is the one he feels, which is an ache like he's never known and a breathlessness that feels like he's dying too.

Death came and now darkness, only darkness—lights out.

He blinks and blinks and blinks again, hoping to regain vision, to regain presence in this harsh moment he has found himself in. For the longest time, nothing. No light returns. No light emerges. No light at all.

Lights out—only mourning, only sorrow, only grief.

And then, slowly, with time, there is a glimmer, a speck of light and hope. He starts to see outlines, shadows showcasing the things left over, the things still here. Light returns, but never the way it was. This light, this new glow, is different. Different in ways that will take time to comprehend as the world has suddenly shifted into something unknown. He has vision again, but his orientation of things has skewed, has blurred.

He realizes this is a moment that will change him, the experience that will require him to see differently. Because now he, in fact, sees differently.

Until now, he never realized how each time in his childhood, in his youth, when a storm would come and the lights would disappear, it was grief's clone, grief's replica, only void of the heartbreak and the loss. He wonders if those storms, those times of darkness, were a test, a trial, to ensure he would remember that the lights always came back on eventually.

He wonders if those dark moments were to teach him that having an absence of light is scary and unnerving and full of unknowns but that the light always resumes, in some way, even though different than before. Ironically, he feels thankful for those subconscious lessons, those intimidating storms.

Because of them, he knows that with time, light must reappear. He's confident that he will one day see past death's total darkness. He's already experienced tiny glimmers, proof of radiance and light. He hopes with time his sight will return, though not the vision produced by his eyes, but the kind that allows him to see through the lens of love and legacies.

And the light will return. He's sure of it.

And it won't fill the void or the empty space. It will not cure his heartbreak or his grief. Light cannot do that.

But it will return. And it will be sacred.

It will be the light of love and legacies. And he looks forward to that shine.

May we all be blessed with the light of love and legacies—lights that cannot be dimmed or darkened. Lights that shine indefinitely, forever.

like a child

He sits at the freshly covered grave, and he wails. Until now, I have never seen him cry. Losing a parent has that effect on you. I would know.

I mourn with him from afar, giving him space. I hear someone whisper, "His cry is like a child."

And I wonder what they mean, what they're insinuating.

Cry like a child—words said with a tone of judgment, a tone of criticism.

I am surprised. I am disheartened. Surely it cannot be. I've heard incorrectly, my ears have failed me like longevity has failed the person he yearns for. Surely, criticism and judgment cannot exist in a space of mourning.

As you stare at the boldest proof of life's fragility, as you witness a life ended—a body buried—can a person be so unsympathetic as to mock grief's consequences, death's fallout?

How naive do you have to be to grief, to death, to watch someone in the pit of ache and condemn their emotions, their heartbreak?

These words were said like a slight, like an insult, but in my mind they appear to be quite the reverse.

Children grieve authentically. They cry without shame. They don't allow the critique or opinion of others to restrain their heart's emotion, their soul's instability.

They let their tears be visible.

They keep their emotions free.

They hold no inhibition about grief or tears because the world hasn't yet told them to.

What if the world never told them to? Never told the child-versions of us to hide our pain and bury our longing? Maybe these people would stand in the midst of mourning with a little more empathy, a little more compassion. Maybe they would stand with hands on shoulders in support, rather than hands holding magnifying glasses searching for weakness, for brokenness.

How beautiful are the tears of a child, not because of what caused them but because of what they represent—the unfiltered permission to grieve honestly and to let tears speak when words cannot.

He sits at that grave speaking in a language those people haven't learned yet. A language of loss. A language of death and life and memories and legacies. A language of unknowns. A language that those of us who have stood on fresh dirt, awaiting a headstone's arrival, understand and internalize.

A language beyond their knowing, unfamiliar, for now.

And I hope one day, when they find themselves weeping on newly turned soil, that they hold the unspoken permission to grieve authentically and let their tears speak when words cannot, as someone in the crowd whispers, "Their cry is like a child."

And it won't be judgment. It will be empathy—only empathy.

I know grief

I know your smile is fake and your strength is limited, that it's reserved for things like breath and the ability to get out of bed each day.

I know your faith feels like a glimmer—here one moment and gone the next. I know the complicated pull between hope and despair, the chaos between belief in heaven and the anxiety and worry of nothingness.

I know your prayers feel lost and your wishes feel ungranted. I know that you feel betrayed, having not received either of them—answered prayers, granted wishes.

I know you wish people understood and also that they'd never have to. You wouldn't wish this emptiness on anyone. You wish it wasn't your truth to hold, your loss to endure.

I know that your body keeps moving and moving and your schedule keeps going and going. All the while your soul feels like it's shattered and the world keeps stepping on the pieces—walking joyfully on your sorrow, on your brokenness, not acknowledging it exists.

I know that you've cried in silence and hidden your grief in places that feel safe—places that have become the sacred keepers of your longing and despair.

I know that you hurt in places you cannot reach, pieces of your being you cannot locate for you didn't know they existed until now.

I know because I forever live with a death, an absence, that still takes my breath away—because I live with grief.

I also know that you're most likely not giving yourself enough credit. A weaker version of you might not have survived this.

But you are.
You endure
and endure
and endure.
And you survive.

You persist even when consumed with darkness, even when consumed with anger or confusion. You persevere through the heartbreak, through the uncontrollable outcomes—and you live.

You learn to continue with both potential and pain, a legacy and a loss.

You learn to live again.
You learn that life, even with grief, is worth living.

I know because
I've lost
and mourned
and grieved
and survived and wanted to.

One day you will too.

Grief is survivable. It's as harsh and as hopeful, as simple and as complicated as that.

You can, and will, survive this.

their legacy

*"Be their greatness. Be their love.
Be their lasting legacy."*

XOX, Chels

a letter they never got to write

Goodbye, I love you.

I'm starting this with goodbye but hoping it becomes so much more—a combination of I love you, I'll miss you, and hopefully all the other beautiful things my heart wants to reveal. You have no idea that I'm writing this, and even worse, no idea that an earthly goodbye is about to find us.

There is no manual to explain to the people you cherish and love the most that you are about to die. There is no class that teaches how to soften the devastation or ease the anxiety. And yet the truth still stands: I am about to die.

I wish I could stay longer, but since that possibility has evaporated, and will continue to dissipate with each coming day, please know that I would have stayed forever if it was a choice. I would choose more each and every time—more laughs, more celebrations, more mundane moments, more of you, more of us—more life.

But more is beyond a miracle, it is an unachievable wish. Instead, I will use what remains to share what I hope you will carry with you—beyond me, beyond my death. Those things are my memories and my love.

I wish I could tell you my favorite hug or kiss or memory, but as I sit reviewing my life, I simply cannot pick one. It was all of them. It was the ability to have all of them. It was the way they became like breath, effortless. It was the way my life was blessed each and every time I got to see you. My best days were the ones with you—always.

Never forget that my biggest blessing in life was you and I hope I remain one of yours.

Promise me that when the casket has been closed and my body has been buried, that you will not also bury yourself—not with grief or heartbreak or my death's aftermath. Do not allow death to multiply, only my legacy and my influence. To honor me, you must keep living. Please, keep living, not merely surviving, but boldly and brilliantly living.

Make sure hope lives as effortlessly in your heart as grief's ache. Keep all of my comfort from the past and use it on days where you feel only the weight of my absence and not the blessing of my memory. When you cannot find hope, create it—just like I always tried to do for you.

Know that some things are limitless and hold no boundaries, even when they cannot be seen or felt in traditional ways. Love is one of those things. Please, never forget that reality. My love for you will never stop—distance and location and even death will not change that truth.

While I wish things could be different, I do not fear what is next for me. I've been living by the promise of heaven my entire life. My only fear is that my death will pause your happiness or that it will change you in ways that harden your heart. Do not allow that fear to become fact. It would feel like an undoing of everything I've tried to teach you.

Please live inspired by me and not for me. My life has been beautiful and breathtaking and imperfect in ways that solidify it was mine.

More than anything, know how loved you are. Know that while you will miss me, I will not have to miss you. I'll be a part of it all in immeasurable and unseen ways. From now on, there will be no coincidence, only love finding you in unique ways. My love will find you, indefinitely.

I love you—always and forever. xox

witnessing legacies

She's a teenager now, about to walk across the gym floor to accept her middle school graduation certificate. She's so beautiful. Every time I look at her, I see a combination of her baby self and the breathtaking young lady she's becoming. She's a mixture of all the influences of those who love her. She's the visual representation of a legacy—hers, mine, and those before both of us.

People ask me all the time what a legacy is. It is this.

A legacy is a life unfolding because of the grit of its owner and the inspiration of those who love them. It's living inspired by others but uniquely designed through individual wisdom and experiences. It is being both your authentic self and also the delicate and delightful things you appreciated about those who are no longer here.

It's living boldly, because you are able to.

It's living with impact, both now and beyond your time on earth.

It's having the kind of heart and influence that people want to replicate, not redesign.

A legacy is this, both the becoming and the attachment to the things that allowed you to become. The gift of your life and all of the lives that led to a ripple effect of your creation—your happening.

I'm in awe of what I'm witnessing. I'm watching the very beginning of a legacy—my daughter's—while simultaneously watching my mother's legacy unfold in new ways, even though she's gone. And even more profound, I'm watching mine open and expand in ways more meaningful than I could have ever imagined.

A legacy isn't an independent or singular thing. It's a collaboration, a combined effort, of both inheritance and creativity.

It's resilient love that empowers.

It's intelligence that enlightens.

It's an outcome that changes an ending into a cycle of influence and remembrance and action that keeps moving things forward—bigger and better with each and every life it touches, including the original inventor.

A legacy is built over time, decision after decision, relationships mixed with relationships, morals and goals and intentions combined. It's theirs and yours, together—an ultimate duality of exclusive and inclusive effect.

As I continue to gaze in my daughter's direction, I realize each one of us is both the recipient of a legacy and also the maker of one. And if we're lucky, we're the recipient of multiple legacies, all gifted with the lives of those who loved us—a final gift, a final delivery and acceptance of sincere love.

I knew eventually I'd become the keeper of my mother's legacy, though it came before I anticipated or was ready for it. I knew I, too, would eventually have a legacy of my own. What I never realized was how I'd have the ability to be a spectator to the exquisite beginnings of my daughter's legacy. I never realized how with each moment that you find yourself caught in the experiences and lives of those around you, you're surprisingly watching the slow unveiling of another's legacy. What a priceless gift that is to witness.

When you glance in the direction of those you love, can you spot their legacy?

Can you visualize your own?

Can you honor and utilize the legacies already placed in your hands—the ones from loved ones passed?

We're all blessed with multiple legacies.
Some to make.
Some to cherish.
And some simply to bear witness to the start of their existence, never knowing how exactly they'll finish.

And I think that's the hope today. May we execute and honor the legacies we're gifted. May we establish and construct legacies that we're proud of. And more than anything, may our children keep creating their own long after we're here to observe.

Who knew we were all witnesses of legacies—many, many, legacies.

ungiven inheritance

My mother's cancer was the kind that could have been coded in my DNA too—inherited from her. Determined by her composition, her genes. Placed inside my creation the same as eye color and height.

How awful a world where a mother is told that she is dying and that her children might be dying too—slowly by the fate of having her cells, her makeup.

My mother had to hold her truth, her outcome, while praying the tests would show it wouldn't be ours, her children's, too. She had always called us her masterpieces, her works of art. Now, she prayed her body worked carefully, only giving the normal and healthy pieces of her.

Suddenly we had to witness a world that gave my mother a fatal cancer diagnosis and then we had to listen as doctors explained that she might have given her kids the same. That I could be the same—terminal.

Blood was taken. Tears wouldn't need to be as they flow effortlessly, easier than the blood, the crimson fluid entering the vial.

For weeks we waited for doctors and scientists to examine my cells, my DNA.

For weeks I prayed for the first and only time to *not* be like my mother. For weeks I'm sure she prayed the same.

And I wasn't.

And we weren't.

My mother's daughters were spared the mutated elements of her body's composition. We were spared from an outcome she couldn't be saved from.

It felt like an answered prayer and also like an unheard and ignored one too.

Us saved. Her contaminated with a disease that would eventually kill her.

And eventually, it did.

She said she knew we'd be okay. And she was right. Her inheritance wouldn't try to kill us. What she couldn't understand was that the death of her would try to.

We survive today because a piece of her was missing in us.

How complicated a truth to hold. Never has an absence of her felt so joyous, felt like such a gift. Especially when we're left clinging to every piece that remains, wanting nothing held back, nothing ungiven.

My mother gave us every single piece of her—*except one*.

The one that would have harmed us.

The one that would have shortened our lives.

The one that shortened her own.

And if that isn't the boldest and most radical push and permission to live, I don't know what is.

She unknowingly saved us. And we will live each day because we can, even when she can't—all because of one tiny piece of an inheritance ungiven.

a moment, not their memory

A flashback comes, I can see my mother lying on the bed where she'd ultimately take her final breaths. Her breathing is so slow it's almost unable to be recognized or noticed. She is frail and the color of her skin is an unnatural shade of gray combined with specks of yellow. She doesn't move. She is still.

Her hair is flat to her head in a way she'd probably be annoyed by if she had the ability to be aware of it. Her eyes are closed, but in my head, I can feel the tears that are trapped underneath. She is my mother, though she looks nothing like the woman I know. She is a different version of herself—the version of herself that is dying. She is barely clinging to life, which is unavoidably evident by the fact that right now, she already looks—

Before I can finish the sentence, before I can conceptualize that last glimpse of a harsh moment in time, I'm jolted back to the current moment. The one where I'm standing alone in my kitchen, now crying from the memories of my mother's death. Now grief-stricken and haunted by the last minutes and seconds of life with the greatest woman I've ever known. Traumatized by the version of my mother I last encountered—the one where cancer had made her body unrecognizable. The one where her impending death changed her glow, her light, and each of her abilities.

And as that vision of my mother continues to bring tears and ache, a gentle thought enters my mind, as if a heavenly whisper from my mother: *That was a moment of mine, a final moment, please don't allow it to become my memory.*

I'm speechless and punched with a perspective that is bolder and more glorious than my own. It hits me like a mist of hope and love—the motherly kind that has protected me most of my life. The kind of solace and comfort I thought I lost when my mother passed.

But now, here in this moment, it has returned like a gift from above, or a blessing from her, or both. Like a dignified perspective shift from brutal pain to beautiful comfort.

It felt like a personal request from my mother—as if in her gentle motherly tone she was saying, *Dear daughter, do not let the vision of me at my earthly end and the heartbreaking and harshest moment of our time together be my memory. Let it stay as a moment, a truth, an experience, but do not let it shape or become my memory.*

Be grounded in love's reminiscence, not pain's nightmare. Envision me in my glory and let me stay there. Remember me locked inside our favorite moments together, not trapped in death's darkness, for that experience was only unsympathetic and cruel for you. For me, it was like shifting to the next thing, the one that lasts forever.

Each and every time that final moment enters your mind, replace it with memories of me at my best. The times when I did something silly. The times when I made a difference in your life. The times when I was happy and smiling because of you. The date on my headstone was a moment of mine, a final moment, please don't allow it to become my memory.

Through sobs, unsure how this message is finding me, I know it has to be her—whether from her directly or through the pieces of her that remain in me. Either way, it's the voice I needed to hear, the message my heart sought comfort from.

If she's asking me to remember her through hope and love, through laughter and happiness, through the infinite influence of faith in the beauty of life and not the pain of death, I will.

I'll remember her—her way—not just now, but always.

May we keep their death a moment, not their memory. And may we all remember them *their* way—forever.

letters & pennies from heaven

Inspired by the Breedlove family

She picks up the pen, ready to write a letter from heaven. Immediately she decides against it as her handwriting is distinguishable and would undo the magic of all she's in pursuit of. This letter isn't truly from heaven, of course, it will be printed from just down the hall in her office. This letter is an extension of love—sent from someone earthside as a reminder of the love and memory of someone in heaven.

The tiny soul it's addressed to doesn't need to know the firm truths of this letter's delivery. For now, she needs to keep her youthful naivety and be continuously wrapped in the comfort, hope, and faith of others, which one day she'll grow into. At least that is the hope, isn't it?

Yes, children are resilient, as the world says, but they experience grief and sorrow too. Because of that, she begins typing:

> *I miss you. Jesus says hello. Heaven is just as the Bible says—perfect. I'm watching over all of you. You're making me proud. Here is a penny from heaven. Watch for more, I'll be sending them often. I love you and I miss you.*
>
> *Papa*

It's the first, but many follow—letters and pennies, pennies and letters.

Both signs of a connection from heaven to here, and here back to heaven, in intentional ways that weave influence and memory from both the living and the dead.

Each time she notices an ache in those youthful eyes, or a longing that cannot be fully soothed, she begins typing. She types, not to deceive, but to actively participate in the truth that love never dies. Instead, it gets delicately transferred from the deceased to the living so that it continues to spread and bless those still here.

Letters and pennies, pennies and letters—continuations of a legacy, reminders of an infinite love, memories of someone unforgettable.

She's never been an author but each one of these letters is her masterpiece. They are her way of ensuring that the unforgettable remain unforgettable, especially in the minds of those whose age can be quickly counted on the tiny fingers of their hands. These letters are her attempt to extend legacies and if she's lucky, to create a presence where an absence has been created.

She writes letters from heaven. The pennies arrive by coincidence. They are found by chance, hopefully right when they are needed. She likes to think that they arrive not by coincidence at all, but through the limitless power of God. She likes to think that these pennies are heaven's way of assisting the project when she can't or isn't able—a continuation of her work.

And each letter is remarkable and profound.

And each letter is deeply appreciated and acknowledged.

And each penny is a visible representation of life's surprises and love's infinite gift.

She realizes through each letter she sends that in attempting to soothe and comfort her granddaughter's soul, she has done the same for her own. Healing her grief wasn't part of the plan, but it has been a treasured outcome. She had no idea that letters and pennies could be one of grief's remedies—not a cure, rather more of a salve, a balm, an aid in healing. What a gift these heavenly messages are—for everyone.

These letters are written to keep the names of those we've lost and the memory of those no longer here engraved in our hearts in ways that cannot be ignored, nor forgotten. She will keep writing until these heavenly sentiments are no longer needed, as the entire goal of these one-of-a-kind letters is to eventually have love and reminiscence ingrained so permanently in our hearts that outside reinforcements and confirmations are no longer needed.

After years of writing these special addressed notes, she realizes that eventually her legacy will be letters and pennies, pennies and letters. She will keep writing these letters from heaven until one day someone will have to write them for her.

Letters and pennies.
Pennies and letters.
Forever—first written by her, then written inspired by her.

She started this project never knowing that one day her legacy would be letters and pennies from heaven.

better for it

We are better because of their life, their love, but we are also scarred by their death. Which one of these truths will shape us most? Which one will give the most influence and the most power? That decision, that one critical choice, will design the lives we live without them—our lives.

It remains true, a reality death cannot erase, that we are better from it—all of it.

Their love, their light, their flaws, their mistakes, their adoration, their pride.

Their everything.

We tell people that we are better because of them.

Are we living in that truth?

Are we living like we're better for it?

Are we living like we'd do it all again, even with the knowing that it would end just as it did, with their deaths harsh and premature?

Are we living like they did, despite pain and grief? The very one we're mourning once mourned others too. Yet they lived. In fact, they lived so beautifully, so grandly, that they inspired, uplifted, encouraged, among so many more formative and indelible things.

Will others feel the same about us? Will they speak that same truth?

Are our own lives, though now filled with holes and pain, still worthwhile and designed with the acknowledgment that life is a gift—the ultimate treasure, a limited offering?

If we are truly *better for it, better because of them*, it will show. It will be evident in everything we do, which means we must *do*. Not just *be*, but *do*. It's actions, not just intentions. It's *living* and *wanting to live*—two very separate things. It's effort and a pursuit with meaning and purpose, most of the time difficult, but always valuable, both for us and those around us.

To be better for it, we have to actually *be* better for it, instead of being burdened by one piece of it, that piece being their death, their end.

So, I ask, *Are you better for it?* And even more critical, more pivotal, *Would I be able to tell?*

keeping things

I kept all of her belongings since I couldn't keep her.

I kept the blankets and her clothes. I kept the furniture and for a while I kept her house too. I couldn't dare give away the only pieces of her that remained. I didn't want others, outsiders, touching or taking things she treasured, no matter how small, no matter how insignificant, no matter how ripped or worn.

I kept the things because I couldn't keep her.

I kept things I couldn't use and things that were broken. Things now shoved in the back corners of my basement, unused and unseen. Of course, I kept all the sentimental things too. Things now kept on display to remind myself and others of her life, of her existence. Those things feel as important as my next breath. I wonder if others in grief have felt the same.

I kept it all so I wouldn't have to let her go—again.

I had no choice in her ending or watching as she died. These things, they are a choice. And I choose to keep them, so she is here, if only in tiny and unconventional ways.

I stare at these things, some big and some small, and I wonder what she'd say if she knew I kept them all—every single thing. Would she laugh? Would she roll her eyes? Would she even care? Would she wonder why I feel so compelled to keep them? I know others often do.

I keep them because they were hers, and after her death they became mine—inherited, gifted.

I keep them because she once held them, once touched them, which means they hold invisible little specks of her presence.

I keep them because at one moment in her life she chose them, maybe for a specific purpose, maybe because they made her smile. Either way she looked at them and said, "I like this. I want this." And so now I do the same.

Or do I?

Do I like them? Do I want them? To most, the answer is no.

I keep things when, really, I wish I could keep people—her. And there is so much ache in knowing that things outlast people. But things, you see, cannot outlast love.

And I think I might be collecting the wrong items, the wrong things.

We keep their belongings thinking it will keep us tethered to them in some tangible way. And while some do, and some can, most cannot. We clutter our lives with material items when we should be filling our lives with their influence and their love.

The most powerful things are not the ones we can touch, but rather, the ones we can carry.

Her belongings, for now, will stay here, tucked away until I find the right place for them. But her lessons, her legacy, those will stay—always. Not tucked away, not hidden in the corners of a dark basement, but lived through me.

And I hope she can see that I kept more than things.

committed

I am committed to having your life be the thing you're remembered for, not your death, not your disease. I will not allow your final days, your final look, to determine the image in minds and hearts—especially mine.

I am committed to ensuring you're never forgotten, not by anyone who knew you. I will share your stories. I will ask for new ones. I will create conversations with those from your past, ones I never knew, to ensure new pieces of you keep being found, keep being uncovered.

I am committed to continuing the traditions that meant so much to you, the ones you worked so hard to both create and carry on. The ones that still fit because you made sure they'd always be meant for us, designed in both your honor and our dreams.

I am committed to you in death the same way I was in life—to make you proud. To make you honored that I am yours. To make you smile and make you laugh. To make you alive in ways that you can no longer create yourself.

I am committed to honoring and listening to your advice, knowing there will be no new suggestions voiced, no new recommendations spoken. When there is nothing left but past guidance, previous feedback, I hold it with greater intentionality and openness.

I am committed to ensuring you're not only a photograph in our wallets. You're the face and influence etched on our hearts and everything we do. You won't be only a memory. You'll be our motivation.

I am committed to the perspective, the truth, that you're more than an empty seat, an absence. You're the invisible presence that follows us with silent whispers of *I love you*. You're more than a name we speak of. You're a life we live in honor of, a soul whose influence remains immeasurable and unwavering.

I am committed to taking care of the things you loved, which includes me. I promise to take care of myself, even when it's hard and especially when it feels like an unwinnable challenge due to grief's weight and exhaustion.

I will live committed to your life and your memory, not consumed by your death. You deserve not only to be mourned but also to be cherished and appreciated and honored in ways that keep your love and influence alive forever.

Your death was not the end of your presence. It was the beginning of your legacy. And I am committed, fully committed, to ensuring it is fulfilled.

Beyond your absence, through your presence, and in the creation of your legacy—I am committed.

they live

She lives. Not in the conventional way but in ways that allow her to still exist. There are many ways to exist, some literal, some creative, some imaginative even. Either way, she prevails beyond death. Existence and aliveness were not stolen from her when her breath was.

She lives.

She exists in the spaces that held her influence. She remains in the beneficial outcomes of her routine intentions, ones that are still impacting lives today. She remains, by memory, in all of the places that were hers, the places she visited again and again. She lives in coincidences and also in recollections and reminiscences.

She lives.
They live.

They live in their favorite spaces. Not literally, in ways that you can touch and see, but certainly in ways that you can feel—which makes them very much alive. Alive through influence, through transformation, through tiny specks of them that shed when they were here.

We hear about DNA being left at crime scenes. We forget it can be left at other places too—joyous places, intimate spaces. Places like church pews. Places like the hands that they held. Places like the chair or seat that was always marked "theirs" so no one else would occupy it. Places like the backyard swing and the wagon they dragged carrying little ones they loved.

Places. They exist in places. And in minds and hearts and photo albums and pictures on the wall. They exist in so many places that you forget about them all.

Do not allow circumstance to make you think death eliminates a life completely. It cannot.

Grief sometimes gives a false sense of power and authority to death. The power truly lies in everything before death arrived. It lies in life—in the guidance and love and legacy of the person who lived it.

They live—through us, through legacies and love.

They live.

continue the conversation

They may no longer be beside us, but we can still continue the conversation. All we have to do is speak.

We can still tell them what's in our hearts.
We can still share our hurts and our worries.
We can still divulge our regrets and our wishes.
We can still spill our secrets and our shame.
We can still celebrate our love and our adoration.
All we have to do is speak.

Speak into the wind and up to the sky.
Whisper to the wilderness. Cry to the clouds.
Vocalize your emotions and your story.

They don't need to be next to us. Eternity's capabilities are endless. There is no prayer, no sentiment, no words that go unnoticed, unacknowledged.

You are noticed. We are noticed, always and forever, even from afar.

Talk to them.

They hear us in ways translated by Jesus and delivered by God.

Talk to them in a language so perfect, so pure, it needs only one thing—you.

Talk to them.

They are no longer next to us, beside us with their presence, but we can still continue the relationship, the conversation.

All we have to do is speak—so speak.

living again

"We cannot allow their deaths to be our caskets—our tombs."

xox, Chels

marked for you

Death handed you grief, not a grave. Did you confuse the two?

The grave is marked for your loved one. The grief is marked for you.

You seem to have attached yourself to soil that has already been packed down, burying the one who passed, the life gone. This space is not for you—only them.

You hold grief but you hold life too.

You get more—
more days.
more breaths.
more heartbeats.
more opportunities.
more everything.
At least for now.

And wouldn't they want you to?

Wouldn't they die ten times over if it presented the opportunity to multiply your days, quadruple your living?

They would.

So, take grief and quit trying to enter the ground of a sacred space, secured for someone else—them.

You hold grief but you hold life too.

The grave is marked for your loved one. The grief is marked for you.

ticking toward purpose

Behind each thing we do today, there is a clock ticking. A clock that marks the days and minutes that are left to be ours. The time that signifies life here on earth and then subsequently life in eternity.

Most days we forget that it's there—*ticktock, ticktock, ticktock*.

Most days we get lost in the schedules, the shuffle of chaos, and the hurry to get to the next thing.

The advancement of the hour and minute hands becomes so incredibly tethered to your days and your perspective when you lose someone you love. Grief not only shows you what happens when time runs out, it also becomes embedded into who you are and how you show up. It no longer gives you the option to forget the fragility of time or the limits to life. Once you witness the sacred moment of life's transition you never look at life the same. You never look at people the same—or time or love or pain.

If you know profound loss, you know the feeling of looking at not just a person but also the sand passing through the hourglass of their life. You know the importance of a moment, so you wonder when it will suddenly be their last. You know the significance of health, so you anxiously analyze the well-being of you and every person you know. It's not a choice, it's a cycle of worry from all the knowing—grief's knowing, grief's lessons.

When you watch a life fade and a clock stop, you're left with profound confusion, an intense fear, and a sadness that attaches itself to emotions like joy and happiness.

Eventually, beyond the freshness of loss and the brutality of death's consequences, you realize that while one clock has stopped, yours is still ticking. You had forgotten about it, but the faint *ticktock, ticktock, ticktock* has slowly gained volume and magnitude. You are still here. You are still alive.

You still have a purpose and plans.
You still have a story.
You still have worth.
You still have things to do.

On hard days you might feel like ripping out the batteries on that clock or taking a peek to see if you can tell how much power and energy are left—but don't. We aren't meant to know our days and our minutes. We aren't meant to be in control of time or life. Our minds cannot comprehend such delicate and sensitive knowings.

Instead, think about the person you've lost. Think about their love and their guidance. Think about their wisdom and their deep dedication and devotion to you—someone they love fiercely.

Imagine them as the mechanic of your clock, the manager of your time. They'd want you to live for as long and as beautifully as you can. They'd want each minute to count and each day to matter. They'd want you to care for yourself, not just those around you. They'd want you to be mindful of each tick and each tock but not fearful of them. They'd want you to live for both you and them.

They'd want you to stay, until you can't stay any longer—until you've vibrantly collected an incomprehensible abundance of ticks and tocks.

Live while you still can. After all, you're living for two—you and them, one a life and one a legacy.

version two: becoming again

There is no going back to the before—before loss, before grief, before all the chaos of those two things combined. There is only the choice to begin again, which is really what life is, a series of beginning again and again and again—indefinitely.

The alternative to beginning again is staying—staying in the pain and the darkness, immobilized by a life changed by things you have no power to correct or undo. Staying is the option with the smallest effort because the weight is easy to buckle beneath and the darkness seems to effortlessly steal the light. Grief becomes so intimidatingly powerful that it can outshine love and legacies if you let it, and it's easy to let it.

To begin again you must battle for flourishing life, not just aliveness. The two are not the same, one is an experience and the other is a cage—a confinement. One is engaging with life, flaws and heartbreak included, but also joy and reminiscence. The other is strictly a means of survival. It's a place that most of us find ourselves at the beginning of grief, but it's one where we aren't meant to linger, for its power grows with each day and each moment. Pain can easily suppress every contradictory thing. The healing comes by not letting it.

There is no going back to the before, but there can be brilliance and meaning and purpose in this new after. Healing doesn't end the longing and the ache, rather it equips us to adapt to them. It helps us see a past to be grateful for and provides us the capacity to hold grief and reminiscence as partners in each thing to come. Healing and grief will now coexist together.

Grief exists effortlessly, causing transformations and unavoidable emotions. Healing is complex and requires effort and choice. Grief comes without an invitation. Healing can only begin with an invitation.

Are you welcoming healing? Are you seeking it? Or are you scared that with healing comes forgetting? Are you worried that with healing comes abandonment of a relationship you're working fiercely to preserve? Are you worried that healing detaches you from the truths of what was and sews you into the unknowns of what is to be, especially when it will not include someone you love, someone you've lost?

It's common to resist a new version, both of life and of you, especially one curated without your consent and without the unique artistry of your desires and creativity. While we may feel like we're the producers of our own lives, through loss and immense pain we learn that life's fragility, grief, and time limitations are also responsible for the designs that impact our days.

It would be easy, almost effortless, to surrender to the pain. It often feels like the best solution. It's certainly the least complicated one. But it's also the place where influence and love cease to exist, for they cannot compete with solitary confinement, caged and unwitnessed.

The hardest thing is typically the most critical thing we need, yet it's the one we most often repel. Are you fighting healing or are you trying to absorb it? Are you willing and ready to soothe the pieces of your soul that have been wounded by grief? Are you ready to be not only a witness but an engaged participant in the unfolding of each new day?

This is your life. Your only opportunity to live. Will you?

Will you choose becoming again and again and again in version two?

waiting

I sink into the couch and pull out my book knowing I'll be waiting awhile, a perk of arriving early. I open my book to the correct page but before beginning I scan the waiting room. Everyone here is silent but busy—scanning phones and reading books. One person is concentrating on a word puzzle, or so it seems.

We're all here, waiting.

Waiting to unleash our brokenness.

Waiting to uncover both our hidden traumas and also the not-so-hidden ones.

Waiting to recover from grief or at least mend in a way that is helpful.

Waiting to be cleansed of the things that are wrong with us, the things wrong with our minds or our souls or all of the above.

We're all here for the same reason—to heal.

For some, we come to find healing, for others we come to continue healing.

Either way, it does not matter. We are here.

I've never realized how therapists' waiting rooms seem like bold HIPAA violations. If you are here, either you need help or someone you love needs help. Either way, it is clear, help is needed. Years ago, this would have detoured me. Time has shifted my perspective and also my vulnerability.

The people here feel safe, though we've only exchanged smiles, never speaking or sharing names. They feel authentic and unapologetic in ways that allow me to sit here, unafraid and unashamed. Sitting here signifies I need help, and I'm okay with that weakness showing because I'm surrounded by others who are willing to do the same.

It's courageous to ask for help, even when you do so out of desperation and exhaustion.

It takes bravery to confront pain. It takes grit to commit to change, especially when the change means moving forward when someone you love no longer has that opportunity.

It means confronting pain instead of avoiding or ignoring it—which means staring at an empty space and promising yourself you won't let it empty you too.

It means letting someone witness your sorrow and your mourning, even though society taught you the opposite and peers showed you that it made them uncomfortable.

It's leaning into the discomfort, even though it's one of the very last things you want to do.

You want to run. You want to hide. You want to isolate.

But you are here, waiting. Or rather, I'm here waiting.

Waiting for the transformations that I'm hopeful will come. Waiting for sorrow to be exchanged for remembrance and mourning to shift from survival to actually living again.

Waiting to be the kind of person whose whole personality isn't grief. Waiting to be more than "the woman whose person is dead." Waiting to be the version of me that will become something, most profoundly a version of me that is healing, a version of me that wants to heal. Waiting to be a woman who doesn't need grief as a badge of honor because love has taken that place.

Waiting for the wisdom to know that contentment is just as powerful and influential as happiness and joy.

Waiting.

I quiet my mind and get back to the sentence in my book that has been patiently waiting for my attention. I look around one last time and I smile, so proud of each person seated in this room with me. We took the first step. We're putting in the work. We're being humble and we're trying.

And I realize, we're not waiting at all, we're *ready*.

Ready to heal.
Ready to mend.
Ready to live again.

And I wonder, *Which one are you?* Are you *waiting*, or are you *ready*?

closure

They told me I needed closure from death, closure from losing someone foundational in my life.

Closure is a myth. It's a package you order that never comes. It's a promise given from those naive to grief and pain.

After grief, I didn't gain closure, I gained openness. Each day opened to new losses, new unknowns. How can you find closure when your world keeps opening to new places, new holes, new pits, and new mountains? There is nothing to close, only things to climb and others to fall into.

Closure is made for temporary things, not death. It isn't the kind and compassionate ending or healing they're explaining or trying to sell. It's a trap, a way to hide your brokenness. It's a false sense of hope, given by those yet to bury someone they love. It's a challenge to make your life happy again, void of pain and heartbreak. It's meant for their comfort, not yours, so that the mere existence of your experiences can't taint theirs.

Closure isn't for *us*, it's for *them*.

Openness is what we were made for. Openness is what we should chase, what we should yearn for. We should strive and journey for the open.

Open hearts, wounded and vulnerable, but still capable of love.

Open conversations, authentic truth tellers of grief's experience so others are less surprised and genuinely less scared to reveal themselves, grief and all.

Open minds, filled with hope and light and faith, ensuring there is more inside than darkness and destruction.

Open eyes, seeing beyond the date of death, the date of stolen dreams and futures, comprehending and embracing the beauty of what remains, and even more profound, the beauty of what existed.

Openness, not closure, is the key, the glimmer of comfort and perspective we need. Grief and loss break us. They shatter us, scattering pieces of us beyond reach. And still, the world yells "heal" as if it's easy. They shout "closure," as if it's the only way to heal. Instead, I hope you hear the whispers of opening and unfolding.

You've already been broken open. Have you ever considered the power and remembrance in staying that way? Staying open, wide open—to healing, to honoring, to remembering, to living again.

Staying open means understanding that there are still things to embrace, to receive, to learn, and to do. Staying open takes bravery and it takes vulnerability, but it leads to more, like breath and light and love and life.

Closure keeps things locked like a cage. Openness allows them to exist, and even better, to multiply, to grow and be known. Closure protects nothing but potential. Openness protects their legacy and eventually your own.

Each day I will dare to remain open, will you?

trampoline

I hop on the trampoline, too old to be here, but hopelessness can have you chasing wishes, chasing unrealistic desires. My bones crack as I jump and jump and jump, hoping. They keep saying I'll bounce back—this is my effort to speed up that process.

As I leap and bounce, I wonder how far back. How high would I have to jump to go back to when she was here—alive?

I bounce and I bounce. I go nowhere but up and down, then eventually I'm nauseous from it all.

Bounce back, they said—but I didn't.

I couldn't.

I can't.

Turns out their words were mere sentiments, glimmers of hope from someone who's never needed it. They said, "One day you'll bounce back."

They meant that *one day they hope I'll be me again*, in ways that don't intimidate them with my sadness, in ways that don't make them feel like grief will invade them too.

I could bounce forever and never find that person, that place. If I believe these outsiders, these complimentary givers of ambition, I will always fail. I will always be chasing an unreachable destination because "back" is extinct. It is past tense only.

Do they not realize the past evaporated with death, now existing only as a memory, as a place you can reclaim and revisit with reminiscence. But you can't live solidly in reminiscence. You must live in the present too.

So, I can jump for as long and as high as I'd like but the goal isn't, and will never be, to "bounce back." The goal instead is to *live forward*.

Living forward involves allowing loss to change me, to guide me, to inspire me, just as her life and love did. *Living forward* is knowing there is a past but not being confined to the pursuit of reaching it again. *Living forward* is realistic, it's achievable. It's a worthy cause.

When they tell you you'll bounce back, do not believe them. They'll bounce back—to a life unaffected by this loss, uninhabited by grief and mourning.

Others may ask us to bounce back. Life encourages us to step forward—holding memory in one hand and possibility in the other.

My goal is to *live forward*.

lost & found

Life—a game of lost and found. The losses hurt but the findings are the hope, the light.

I yearn for the findings—the glimmers of the deceased, the reminders of their love and their continuation.

We lose them in death, and then
again
and again
and again
in each new day, each new experience.

And in the midst of grief and pain, we find them.

We find them in coincidences,
in the signs.
in the reminders.
in the memories.
in others and in us.

We find them
in butterflies and in birds.
in hope and in faith.
in clouds and in influence.
in every place they once were.
in everything.

We lose their physical presence, and we confuse that truth with permanent absence. The two are not the same.

Finding lost loved ones is easy when you realize they're not lost, not gone.

They remain for we are their continuations—their living continuations.

We remain, and in return, they continue through us—always.

So I ask you, *Who will you find today? And where will you find them?*

The lost can be found.

The lost can be found.

life outlives looks

She tells me that her first thought, always, when walking into a room is what others will think and say about her body.

Will they think she is fat?
Will they think she is ugly?
Will they think she is both?

I used to be like her, worried about my worth through the lens of others' opinions. I know that chase, that desire, to be either acceptable or invisible. Anything else is uncomfortable, terrifying.

She asks what it takes to erase the search for value and acceptance in others, especially in strangers and people she's never met.

I tell her death.
I tell her grief.

I tell her that when you witness a life end, you immediately have a shift in what things are important and which things should be measured.

You learn that health and time and love are the things you want most, the things that matter.

When you see how looks and beauty cannot save you from a terminal illness and how a smaller waist doesn't add time to your lifeline, you start to merit those things less. You start to realize that winning the lottery means living to reach old age, and your loved ones getting to do the same.

When you watch someone lose their life you realize life itself is what makes you worthy and blessed.

I tell her, as a woman, that she'll probably always be up and down, a seesaw of self-confidence and self-doubt. I tell her grief and life's fragility teach her self-compassion.

I tell her my hope is that she'll eventually walk into a room and her first thought will be *thank you!*—thankful for the opportunity to walk into new rooms and new experiences. Not everyone gets that opportunity today or tomorrow or the next days to come. Each door she can open, each room she can walk into, is a gift. A gift of extra days, extra life.

We are here, walking through doors.
We are here, alive.
We are here, just as we're meant to be.

Walk into every room and live.
Live fully and confidently and proud.

And may you count your breaths and your heartbeats more than you ever count calories or the pounds on a scale.

Time shrinks effortlessly each day. Let's try not to shrink our lives more—let's live.

full potential

Her *memory* reminds me that life is filled with possibilities but no guarantees. It reminds me to be purposeful in both my days and my actions.

It's the perspective she'd want me to have—that life is still good, but also that it is limited. That life is for living because there will be a day when it shifts from life to death, from death to eternity.

Her *influence* pushes me to dream big and to take risks. It tells me, just like she once did, that *no* simply means—*next opportunity*.

That the only finality, the only end, is not something the world gives—but rather God and the passing of time.

That faith can be challenged. That it can be imperfect and complicated, but it cannot be gone or taken. It waits patiently for both your questions and your frustrations.

That the most holy and faithful people in the world are the ones who have endured and endured and endured, yet they remain hopeful and helpful, compassionate and kind.

Her *legacy* reminds me of all of our loved ones, the ones from before—the ones she lost, the ones who lost others, yet they persevered. They kept going. They lived their own lives to the fullest potential, even with grief and heartbreak and devastation.

Her memory and her influence and her legacy delicately shout from the heavens that I should be living to my life's full potential. We all should.

Our lives are messy but at the end, they're a masterpiece—our masterpiece.

Their memory and influence and legacy
remind us to—
endure.
experience.
dream.
hope.
feel.
love.
live.

Their life *showed* us. Their memory *reminds* us. Their legacy *inspires* us.

And the hope is that one day our lives and our memories and our legacies do the same.

Will they do the same?

going & going

We know we're not doing well. We know we are struggling. We know that grief is weighing us down and that heartbreak is exhausting us.

And yet, we continue to—
Make the dinners.
Plan the celebrations.
Schedule the appointments.
Organize the extracurriculars.
Handle the tantrums that are not ours.
Continue on and on and on in each new day—for them, for everyone.

We continue to do it all. We push through, never giving ourselves the time it takes to catch our breath, and certainly never the time it takes to heal.

We keep going
and going
and going
and going—
for others.

While what we need is help. Help we don't know how to ask for and help we don't truly know how to identify.

Help to pause.
Help to inhale and exhale.
Help to say no when we're not strong enough.

Help to stop running so we can comprehend it all.

Help to remember that this life is the only one we get.

Help to encourage us to want this life, even when it feels like it doesn't want us.

Help we cannot ask for because we've been taught not to burden others with our problems, with our grief.

Help.
We need help.

And instead, we hide our tears behind shower curtains, and we save our grief for places we enter alone. We show up with smiles that make other people think we're okay. We make it seem like we've turned brokenness into beauty because we've collected our shattered pieces and buried them along with the person we lost.

We persist though we are hurting, though we are mourning.

We persist because it's the only way to show others that they can persist.

We persist because we have to.

We keep going
and going
and going
and going
for others—
until one day we start going for ourselves.

And maybe that's what healing is—starting because of others and continuing because of ourselves.

It was never the brokenness that needed turning to beauty.

It was the nothingness.

We grieved with nothing but ourselves and we made something beautiful out of nothing—we made a life, our life.

faith

"Faith was her strength. I keep asking, Will it be mine?"

XOX, Chels

resilient faith

Some hold an unshakable faith. Mine has been through metaphorical earthquakes and storms—shaken and shaken and shaken.

Does it make me less holy, less Christian, less worthy, if my faith is endlessly complicated and occasionally fickle?

Faith lives inside me. It guides me like a moral compass and inspires me like the divine blessing it is. And yet, sometimes grief and life's heartbreaks create an inner conflict of hurt mixed with belief, mixed with fear and frustration.

If faith is a sacred language, an earned inheritance, am I worthy of its glory if it sometimes has me screaming in wonder, in ache, and in confusion and fear? If I've doubted, if I've held a lack of trust, has my faith failed? Have I?

Can I survive my mind's challenges and silent wars?

If the entire goal is to trust beyond boundaries and to lean in without pulling away, what happens if I've done both?

Can you enter heaven with faith less like a rock and more like water? My faith flows in waves of strength and in waves of questions, while others' faith remains strong and unbreakable. I am breakable.

They tell me that faith is the lifeline and the anchor.
They tell me that faith is the light and the shelter.
It's the bridge to anywhere and everywhere.
It's roots and wings at the same time.
It's a shield and a challenge to live, despite earthly hardships.

It's belief without proof—trusting what you cannot see and what you sometimes do not feel.

For me, in this moment of grief and mourning, faith feels like a mountain I keep trying to climb only to fail halfway up. It feels like a ladder leading to somewhere everyone else can reach, except me. And I can't tell if it's because I'm afraid of stepping off the ladder or if it's because I'm unsure where the next step leads. Or even still, if I'm worthy of the ladder, the climb.

I want a faith that can save me.
I want a faith that's holy and compassionate and full of everything I lack.

And maybe wanting is the first step.

Maybe my faith will never be the rock.
Maybe it's meant to be the tree—
resilient,
constantly growing,
adaptable,
and able to endure endless seasons of change and the unpredictable elements and still survive.

Some people hold an unshakable faith.
I hold a resilient one.

they got to go early

They weren't taken too soon; they got to go early. They were given the gift to see heaven in advance of our expectations so that they could be cleansed of their debilitating disease and unwavering pain. They were given a miraculous blessing that to us felt more like torture, a curse, but to them felt like freedom and the transition they always hoped for.

They weren't taken too soon.
They left ahead of time—our time.
Not theirs. Or God's. Ours.

When their quality of life started to diminish and their ability to live beautifully became more of a miracle than a reality, they were handed an early release—from suffering and agony and things we cannot comprehend, things out of our control. When it felt like they were being ripped from our lives, mercilessly, they were being delicately transferred to a place void of hardship and affliction—a place they prayed they'd be worthy enough to see and blessed enough to experience.

They weren't taken too soon, even though it feels like it.

They shifted their time on this side of heaven for time that is immeasurable because the limit of its possibility does not exist, which is the entire hope and faith of God and eternity.

When their absence feels unsurvivable and their death seems haunted by only suffering and darkness, find hope and light in their faith and their valiant determination to gain glorious and sacred heavenly perpetuity.

Earthly life wasn't stolen from them, even though it feels as if they've been brutally heisted from you and your future. Their heavenly transition doesn't make the grief from losing them less or the pain from "never again" obsolete, but it can comfort our hearts and our days if we let it.

If we allow ourselves to see things from a view beyond our own, that is where we will find the beauty of faith's promise. That is where we will see the freedom and the healing, their freedom and their healing. That is where we will find the selfless courage to hold fierce and fickle grief, knowing that the only things they now hold are joy and exhilaration.

When you know where their future has led, how can you be discouraged by it?

If given the choice, you'd have chosen what was best for them, which is exactly what God has done, even if you cannot accept it or comprehend it, and even when you haven't been able to agree with it.

When you know their fate, truly and deeply, how can you be heartbroken by it?

Sure, your heart and soul ache with the reality of what you are left with, a void, a hole, but when you allow yourself to embrace *their* future and reality, you find solace in it. Not in your circumstances and experiences but in theirs.

Instead of being shattered by their death, we should be moved and inspired by their life. Instead of being tormented by their earthy ending, we should be comforted by their heavenly welcoming.

We hold the loss. We hold the pain. They hold only sacred liberation.

They weren't taken too soon.
They got to go early.

They left ahead of time—our time.
Not theirs. Or God's. Ours.

What a beautiful thing it must be for them to go ahead, to go early—to health and freedom and perfection—to heaven. For now, we hold the grief and the ache. We hold the burden. But one day, we'll hold the beauty of them, already there, waiting for us—all because they got to go early.

eyes closed

He is too young to have seen bodies in caskets and graves with the names of people he's loved, but he has. I can't prevent a reality, a truth, that already exists, though every day I wish I could.

Some of his naivety was lost before he was even born. He would enter this world with a mother who had already buried her own, which meant from his first breath he would be attached to grief too.

He is kind and compassionate and inquisitive. He asks questions we can't answer and also ones that we can.

He asks about heaven.

He asks about angels.

He asks about the truths of bodies that have been buried beneath the earth. He asks if you can take planes to reach heaven or if, when it's our time, the dead come back to carry us there, like some kind of sacred welcoming.

He asks and he asks and he asks.

And out of all of the serendipitous questions he's spoken, there is one that remains the most surprising and significant—he asks, "How do they watch over us from heaven if their eyes are closed?"

What a question.

What a wonder.

He hasn't learned the limitations of bodies or the wonders of souls. Like us, he can't comprehend the beauty of a heavenly presence because he's never witnessed one. He envisions a casket, filled with a body, eyes shut, arms crossed.

He pictures the end as he knows it, as he's experienced it—eyes closed, casket closed.

Sometimes there are no answers for questions so profound, so monumental. Sometimes there is only perspective to meditate on and to ponder.

I wonder if we close the eyes of the dead because if we kept them open, they'd provide a glimpse into the perfection of heaven, a peek into the truths and miracles of God. Do souls and spirits have no use for eyes because they inherently see the goodness of God—the goodness of eternity? Would keeping their eyes open reveal all of these wondrous secrets?

How do you explain to a child, one so small that he can count all of his birthdays on one hand, that heaven isn't bound by limitations like peripheral vision? That eyes in heaven are built by God's design—a design so miraculous it's enhanced to perfection, leaving nothing out of range, no distance exceeding its limit.

He asks, "How do they watch over us from heaven if their eyes are closed?"

And all we can eventually whisper is, "Their eyes are closed in their casket, so we are the very last things they see before opening them in the face of Jesus. We remain the last thing they viewed before witnessing and experiencing the sacredness of heaven. Their eyes were only closed temporarily, to preserve our memory, the way it was down here. From heaven, they'll see us in bold and beautiful new ways. Their eyes are open in heaven—always open, with love."

And I realize that I was once given the profound opportunity, the priceless gift, to be the last thing someone saw before they entered heaven.

Me, then Jesus.

And now my eyes are open, differently than before, all because he asked, "How do they watch over us from heaven if their eyes are closed?"

don't worry, I made it home

It didn't matter that we lived in a small town with speed limits under 50. She'd still get nervous every time I placed myself in the driver's seat of that old green Ford. If it was a late night, she'd be waiting in the living room. On lucky nights, she'd have drifted off to sleep, awoken by the creak of the front door and my gentle, "Don't worry, Mom. I made it home."

By the time college came, I knew the way to ease her worries—a quick call to let her know I was safe and that things were going great. She always wanted me to have roots and wings, but now that I did, it was harsher on her heart than she anticipated. The time didn't matter, all she wanted to hear every now and then were those five simple words: "Don't worry, I made it home."

Through the years, there were many "Don't worry, I made it home" calls and texts and emails. Time and advances in technology changed our communication, but it never changed the message or the comfort that followed. It was our language of love and relief, our language of care. It was an intentional message that told our hearts to rest and our souls to calm.

As years came and went, adulthood found me and so did the necessity to know she was also safe and sound. Time and experience made me wiser, no longer naive to the worry and anxiousness of the world and its consequences. No longer lacking the wisdom and experience to comprehend that life is fragile and time is limited. Eventually, I needed the reassurance of our message.

I needed her "Don't worry, I made it home" calls too.

Through her doctor's appointments and diagnoses.

Through her chemo.

Through her late evening drives or the times when I knew she was drained and exhausted.

Through the times when her will was stronger than her stamina.

I'd anxiously wait for the phone to ring and her voice to say, "Don't worry, I made it home."

And sometimes she'd forget, and other times she wouldn't be quick enough, so I would call her. I would check in. And we'd laugh at how life had changed and roles had reversed. And we never stopped with the dual, "Don't worry, I made it home."

And then, for her, life started fading and time became obsolete. She became too drained to wait up for my calls or messages. She became too weak to drive and too pained to go anywhere farther than the halls of home and the hospital bed that had been delivered there. She no longer waited for my "Don't worry, I made it home," and I no longer needed one from her, for she remained in the same space, usually with me seated beside her.

The kind of comfort I needed now extended beyond our usual language, for now it needed answered prayers and miracles that would never come. Death was impending and approaching quickly. It was about to find her.

And before we were ready, and before we were prepared, her final moments on earth passed. She transitioned from our mother to a memory.

And I feared I'd never again have to say or hear, "Don't worry, I made it home."

Until one day, seated on freshly packed dirt, too early for a stone to be placed on this significant space, I cried in despair and in ache. I begged for her voice, and I prayed for her presence.

And I heard, whether heavenly or coincidentally, "Don't worry, I made it home."

And a wave of unwavering solace rushed over me. Our message, our comfort, had found me again in the most brilliant and profound way. And I believed it. I felt it.

She was home, in heaven.

She was in the most sacred, safe, and special home there is—the forever and infinite one. The one filled with gloriousness and divine beauty and care.

And with both a broken heart and a hopeful one, I whispered, "Welcome home, Mom. Welcome home."

And still, on most days, I look up and whisper, "Don't worry, I made it home," and I know she already knows.

come away with me

As they lay on their deathbeds, wherever that might be, location only an insignificant detail, I imagine them leaving life behind, leaving us behind, as they are welcomed to eternity. Our perspective full of pain, theirs void of it.

As their eyes close for the very last time, they are suddenly met with the faces of the most sacred and holy duo—the faces of God and Jesus. I imagine my toughest "goodbye" being their most blessed "hello."

And whether out of hope or faith, I imagine them hearing—

Come away with me to healing and peace and perfection.

Come away with me to your final destination, your eternal dwelling, one made of only greatness and pure and effortless love.

Come away with me to the place you've prayed for your entire life.

Come away with me where my will stands firm and my promises fulfilled. To a place with unity like you've never known and flawlessness like you've only dreamed.

Come away with me, to heaven.

Come away with me knowing you'll leave the people you love behind while also being reunited with all of those who came before you. You'll be joined in the kind of reunion that lasts forever, the kind that is permanent, the kind blessed and designed by me.

Come away with me without fear and without hesitation, for there is nothing to be afraid of. This will be the easiest and most intentional transformation you endure. You will become the best version of yourself, the one that I created to last forever—a renewed creation.

Come away with me, to heaven.

And they do. They leave for heaven.

And we stay.

And we hope that one day when our time on earth has expired, we will also hear, *Come away with me.* And then, hopefully we'll hear, "I've been waiting for you. You're going to love it here."

And we will love it there—in heaven, with both them and Jesus.

For now, we wait, and we feel grateful for their opportunity to be healed, to be at peace and redeemed, and more than anything for the blessing of them hearing, *Come away with me.*

trust me

I was little. The kind of little where only certain memories are retained from such an age. The pool held most of those memories. It was my family's favorite spot. It held magic, both because it had a curvy slide, which felt like luxury back in the day, and also because it was at my Mémère's house.

I learned to swim in that special pool, clinched tightly to my mother's smooth and gentle arms, staring at her smile. I can still see her poufy hair and her glistening eyes the way they were back then. She knew how important this skill was, so she'd just keep repeating, "Trust me. I've got you and you've got this. Trust me."

And I did.

She'd do the same years later when I was ready and enthusiastic to ride a bike. I was terrified of blood. I gripped the handlebars tight, fearful of skinned-up knees and freshly broken bones. I was scared of both falling and failing. She'd run alongside my bike until just the right time, then she'd give a push and say, "Trust me. You've got this. Keep going. You're doing it. Trust me."

And I did.

High school passed and college came and all throughout my teens she'd find times to say, "Trust me." I didn't always think her ways were just or her opinions grand, but I did *trust her*. I didn't always understand her answers or comprehend her plans, but I always, unwaveringly, *trusted her*.

I'd grow up and become an adult, though I never truly felt like one. I'd call her for mundane advice and answers to things I should have probably already learned or retained. And on one completely ordinary day, she showed up with a "trust me" that would change it all, both her life and mine.

She had cancer. She'd be okay. "Trust me."

And I did.

She went into remission. She was healed. "Trust me."

And I did.

Another cancer came. Another treatment plan. "Trust me."

And I did.

And then, "I'm going to die. I'm not scared. Things will be okay. Trust me."

And I wanted to, but I couldn't. I didn't know how.

And she died, unafraid and in full trust of heaven and God, praying that I'd *trust her* one last time, just like she was doing with the Lord. Her final act of trust was boldly leaning into death—praying it would lead to heaven, knowing it would lead to heaven.

She wanted me to trust her, that her faith was accurate and her belief was pure. She wanted me to trust her and also to trust in God and his plan. She wanted me to trust both of them.

And when I felt like I wouldn't be able to do that, to fulfill her final request for me, I bent down and desperately prayed. I cried. I wailed. I wept.

And in the gentlest whisper, whether in hope or in faith, I heard:

Trust me—your mother is safe and free. Her prayers have been answered. She's watching her faith come to fruition just as she's watching you from places too beautiful to describe. Trust me, in all of your days, just as she did. Trust her and in return you'll trust me too. Trust me.

And I did.

And I do.

It wasn't easy and it wasn't a straight line of achievement, but I leaned in and I learned how. And I trusted.

I wholeheartedly trust my mother—*still, always, forever*—which means now, I trust God too. Just as she taught. Just as she encouraged. Just as she hoped.

She said, "Trust me." And I did.
He says, *Trust me.* And I do.

Do you?

more for you

I used to wonder why God didn't want more for you. Heaven knows I did; we did.

I used to wonder why he didn't want more for you here, on earth, because I did and still do. I think we'll always want more for you, here, with us.

Grief has a way of stealing your faith and also your perspective, it certainly stole mine. One day I sat in prayer and thoughtful meditation, and I asked God the questions that had been filling my heart since the day you left—*Why didn't you want more for her? Why didn't you plan and give her more—more healing, more time, more chances to love and be loved, more of everything?*

His answer didn't come immediately, but one day it did come.

Faith and hope and love ignited me with a perspective beyond pain and heartbreak, and graciously beyond grief. And again, with a more open heart, I asked God—*Why didn't you want more for her? Why?*

And as if my prayer was answered with a silent but intentional whisper that only I could hear, I listened as I heard—

I didn't just want more for her. I wanted everything for her.

I wanted healing and time and love and freedom. Not the kind bound by the limitations of earth but instead the kind promised through my love and my infinite abilities.

I wanted more for her, not just now—forever.

And I believed him. And I believed the message.

And though my "more" is different, I still want it.

But only God has the flawless capabilities of forever. And she undoubtedly deserves the more of infinity and forever. The more of heaven. The more of him.

I'll always wish she had more here—with us. But I also love her enough, and I'm selfless enough, to know which one never ends, and it's only the more of heaven, the more of him.

I want more for her, always.

Lucky for her, God did too.

And lucky for me, for us, God wants more for not just her, but everyone.

More for her.
More for me.
More for you.
More—from him.

imagine heaven

I imagine heaven, not in reality but in my mind. I attempt to stop my thoughts, the ones that replay her death, and instead imagine the outcome that exists beyond my pain. I imagine her truth, her perspective, instead of only my own.

Imagine heaven. Imagine its beauty and its flawlessness. Imagine the way it exchanged her lack of health for unlimited health, the way it transformed her hurt to freedom and her exhaustion to unlimited strength. Imagine how things ended, for her, in the place she fiercely prayed she'd finish.

Imagine heaven, the place that filled her with hope each and every day of her life. The place she learned about and then taught about. The place, not of dreams but of the realistic promises of God. The place, the only place, worthy of her finality.

Imagine heaven, not as a faraway place but as the very atmosphere that surrounds us, one day absorbing us completely, if only we believe. Even if a hope, even if a dream, it makes her feel closer. It makes heaven feel closer.

Imagine heaven for its comfort and its light and its love.

Imagine heaven, in all of its glory, in all its peace and perfect joy, and then imagine her there.

Imagine heaven. She wants nothing more.

Imagine heaven, for her, through her lens. And when you picture her there, and see her fully healed, you'll realize there is no better place or location you prefer. And one day, you think maybe you'll imagine heaven for more than her—you'll imagine it for you too.

Imagine heaven.

And suddenly you do.

You imagine heaven—no longer as a myth but as a promise that is true.

Imagine heaven, first for her, next for you.

Imagine heaven.

found god

I found God on the ground of the cemetery as I wept. He placed a hand on my shoulder and told me that I was okay. He told me that she was okay, though gone, though out of reach.

His touch calmed me. His presence surprised me. His words comforted me.

He softly spoke and promised me that the faith that sustained her saved her completely on the other side of heaven, the glorious place she now resides. He challenged me to lean on that faith, to make it my own, like it had once been hers. He reminded me that long ago she made that choice too.

He reminded me that faith is a choice. He is a choice. Heaven is a choice.

He found me collapsed in despair in a time when I couldn't even find myself. He listened to my anger. He listened to my fears. He listened to my dislikes and all of my questions. He listened and listened.

He found me wounded by grief and radiating mistrust and judgment, and still, he stayed. He stayed, which is how I authentically found him, not from looking or by a search, but in being open to a presence that was most likely always there. He allowed me to find him, though it felt like he had found me, which allowed me to listen to his words and his promises and accept them as my own.

He met me where I was, encountering me in a way not many others did or would do. He wholeheartedly accepted me as I was.

He accepted my mess, my ache, and even my hidden inner chaos, pieces of me that held shame, pieces I thought would render me worthless. He told me I could never be worthless, only priceless. I sat in disbelief.

I found God, thinking it was because he had finally found me. Only he'd been here all along—waiting to be found, waiting to be wanted. Waiting to be the way, my way, by choice and not by authority.

He let me find him when I was ready, not when I was forced.
It changed my grief. It changed my heart. It changed my hope.
It changed my life.

And now I find him everywhere—always.
And I trust him too.
Do you?

what do you believe?

He stands at the podium and asks the church, "What do you believe?" I'm holding the pages of the proof of what I believe in my hands. We all are. His question confuses me.

He continues, "I am not asking what you've been taught to believe or what I'm teaching you to believe. I'm asking for the real and the vulnerable and the imperfect beliefs in your heart and your mind and your soul."

He challenges us to write down what we believe. It took me a few days, but this is what I wrote:

I believe in God.
I believe in Jesus.

I believe in the power of prayer even in times when it hasn't given me the requested outcome.

I believe in goodness and imperfection and that everyone is both.

I believe that a challenged faith, a questioned faith, has the ability to become a resilient one.

I believe that coincidence is only a human word and truth. I believe that God lives in the serendipitous experiences we call chance.

I believe that miracles exist, even though people I love have never been given one.

I believe that love can heal things and so can Jesus and that sometimes healing happens on the other side of heaven.

I believe that faith is personal, and you have to find it, and want it in each new day.

I believe in the trust and faith of my mother, and all of the faithful souls before her, all of the lives that led her to God and church and belief.

I believe in the beyond—
beyond comprehension.
beyond understanding.
beyond earth and everything.

I believe in paths and plans, even when they're still being constructed, still being written.

I believe that light always returns, love always persists, and that death isn't the end to the story.

I believe in the power of small faith, large faith, hidden faith, and upcoming faith too.

I believe the most important thing is to believe.

And just like my mother, I believe if I live out my faith with grace and compassion and encouragement and forgiveness and empathy, others will believe too.

I believe. I truly believe. Do you?

my legacy (& yours too)

"First you held a legacy. Now, you're creating one—one that has the potential to shape generations."

XOX, Chels

what is a legacy?

What is a legacy? It's the baton being passed to the next generation, to someone next in line—not always by blood but invariably and at all times by love. It's life stopping for one body, while another continues into the path that's meant for them, one that still has opportunities and tomorrows. It's each holder, each person, having a stake and a chance to do something with what has been given combined with the call to create and originate new things for all that is to come.

It's a collaborative project of influence meant to last forever.

What is a legacy? It's a continuation of the lives of people you never got to meet mixed with the lives of people you knew and loved well—the most important, the most significant, being the one who gifted you the baton. Because it is a gift to hold the baton, to have the ability to carry it, to continue its work, and to build upon what has already been constructed.

Even the definition itself calls it a gift—do you recognize it as one?

Legacies are meant to be treasured and appreciated, but also continued—built stronger by each generation, each new lesson and experience acquired. So, are you? Are you running with the baton or only holding it? I hope it is the first. I'm sure their hope was the same, especially since they designated you out of everyone.

It was choice, not coincidence, that has you holding the leadership and the responsibility.

Legacies are made from a continuous flow of holders and passers. They are made from the consistent choice to live so intently that it inspires others, especially those we love. They are made from the choice to both receive and then to eventually relinquish benevolently.

Legacies are made by them, by you, by those still to come.

There is no greater gift of love than an inherited legacy.

There isn't a more monumental mission than to both design a legacy and also be one.

So, what is a legacy? It's you. It's them. It's your children and your children's children. It's being someone's legacy and then becoming one.

For now, we hold the baton, we run with it and remain in a pursuit to create something worthwhile. Eventually, we'll pass it on, hoping we did all we could to make it one worth holding.

We are their legacies until we one day become the legacies of the future.

Whose legacy are you? And more importantly, who will become yours?

please tell them my name

One day when I'm only a memory, a face in a photo, please keep saying my name. Ensure I am remembered. Not only by you but also by them and the ones who will follow—the ones I'll never get to meet.

Make my love and my memory so alive, so real, that it seems like they've known it themselves.

Please tell them my name.

Tell them my stories.

Tell them I once was, and will hopefully forever be, a piece of you, which means a piece of them too.

Show them every photo of me that you can find, even the ones I despised, the ones I didn't want to take. Show them the pictures, not to make them sad for what they've missed, what you're now missing, but to reminisce in ways that show them the experiences and moments of the person who now watches them from heaven.

Teach them that I'm still loving you and also loving them from heaven.

Please tell them my name, not only by speaking it but also by the way you live your life. Live so that they know the exact moments when I'm your influence and your guide. They'll recognize the times when my love and my impact have ignited your actions. The hope is that they'll think it's beautiful. I know I will.

Don't pretend I'm something I wasn't. Tell them the truth about me, that I was flawed and imperfect but someone who let love guide every decision I made, even when the reasons and the outcomes weren't understood. Tell them the times I made you mad and the times my faults were on full display. I hope it makes them laugh. I hope it gives them permission to make mistakes and to apologize when it's due.

Please do not live for me, live inspired by me. Live so that my name is sealed in their hearts and souls because they see me through you. The hope is that one day they'll want to do the same.

Please be my legacy, knowing I want it to be wanted, chosen, and not something handed down and seen as only a responsibility. I want it to be viewed as a treasure, not something so insignificant it gets tucked in the corners of a secret closet, forgotten. I want it to be visible, always. And after a million tomorrows, and years and years away, I'll know my legacy was successful when we're in heaven together, and they recognize not just you but me too.

You are my legacy. They are yours.

When I'm gone, please tell them my name and remember me.

future pages

When you write the pages of your future and you delicately ensure the deceased are tucked inside, carefully included, that is a legacy honored and cherished. That is a life ended but never its influence—their influence.

It's ensuring their names are still written on the pages as if they're current characters, not reduced to ghosts. It's each chapter, etched with memory and remembrance, that carries their life forward, carries their life beyond.

They handed us a legacy and when we pick up a pen, we will write *our* futures but *their* souvenirs.

People who assume their aliveness was discontinued with death haven't witnessed you living—in honor of the lost, in action of the lost. They haven't picked up the pages. They haven't read the chapters. If they had, they'd see that those whose names are carved in headstones are still written in our stories as if they were never lost, as if they were still here, just as alive as their memory.

Names mentioned.
Lives remembered.
Souls talked about.
All so alive, so infinite.

They'd hope that one day they'd be written in future pages too. Just as you also hope to be written, to be remembered, intentionally and purposefully.

You look up to the heavens and make promises that lost lives will be remembered and their names will make it to the future in ways they never could.

You write with love.
You write with resilience.
You write with grief and with truth.
You write with an aliveness for all of you—the living and the deceased.

The future can never be empty of them, of us, if we continue to be written in the pages.

And that is their legacy and eventually yours—a future that includes you in the pages.

unfiltered legacy

I don't want my faith to be my golden ticket. I want it to be my yellow brick road, guiding me to all of the places I'm supposed to be, all the spaces that I was made for.

I don't want my legacy to be designed like a luxury brand. I want it to be stitched into a handmade quilt of meaningful pieces. A quilt that allows others to be comforted under its layers, knowing immediately that it was crafted carefully with love and sweat and many things in between.

I want my memory to be unedited, vastly different from the filtered images of today. I want to be remembered for who I am, truthfully, realistically, and not for what filters blurred me to be.

I want my life's truth to be what stays and not some glorified version of me—void of flaws, lighting up rooms that I never walked into, creating smiles that my influence never touched.

Tell the truth about me—all of it.
The funny.
The chaotic.
The messy.
The glorious and the glamorous.
The shameful and the sentimental.
All of it.

I want my eulogy to say I mattered because I made others feel like they mattered. I want my obituary to say I helped and loved and made a difference—a meaningful and positive difference.

Keep my legacy tethered to the legacies before me, never breaking the strand of wisdom, tradition, and inheritance, ensuring mine is one day combined with theirs and leaving space for those who follow. Hoping that others will follow—beautiful and unfiltered combined legacies.

secrets

Grief is a secret we keep from our children. We hide in closets to shelter their hearts from our tears and pain.

We don't want them to see, to learn, that life can hurt. That love can be lost to death. That people die, and even worse, die prematurely, before old age—unlike what we hope, unlike how we pray life will end.

We try to shield our children from a truth that we're trying to survive and outlast and endure. We hope that if we confine our sorrow to the bathroom floor, to unseen spaces, that it won't invade them too.

One day they will be forced to witness grief's consequences. For now, for as long as we can, we keep them naive, we keep them whole.

We hold our grief like we do the realities of the tooth fairy or Santa. We know one day they will find out, that things will be revealed, but we stretch the uncovering out as far as we possibly can.

Save their hearts.
Protect their hope.
Preserve their happiness.
Our silent war cry, a parent's selfless plea.

And we try. We so desperately try.

But grief isn't good at staying hidden, going unnoticed. Grief isn't okay with being a secret when its dream is to be both a lesson and a reminder.

A lesson of life's importance, life's meaning.
A reminder that grief only exists because of love.

We hide, but they know we hurt. And instead of learning that grief is normal, that sadness is okay, they internalize that tears should be concealed, and that hiding and pretending are better than vulnerability and certainly better than brokenness.

Grief cannot be a secret. It should be a tutorial, a lesson, like riding a bike. It's intimidating but it can be done. And once you learn it, you never forget how. And eventually, you must teach someone else.

Grief needs to be lived and observed just like we learn and comprehend love and faith and science and relationships.

Grief is a relationship—a connection to a life gone but a love and memory that remain.

Grief will no longer be a secret that I keep from my children. It will be the truth I live to show them—

Grief is okay.
Sadness isn't shameful.
And loss is limitless.

They will learn that grief is love and that love is never a secret. They will learn grief is welcome here, always welcome.

atoms

I read an article that detailed a new finding of scientists: an atom can exist in two places at the same time.

I saved the link, then printed out the article. I am saving it for the day when I've passed and the world tells you that I'm gone, that I'm lost.

I want a concrete reminder for you that I'll always be both here and there—with you and in forever.

Some will call this hope.
Some will call this faith.
Some will call this wishful thinking.

You can call it truth.

I always knew the capability of being in two places at once. I always knew I'd go someplace holy and also stay here in delicate and unique ways. I was confident because my mother once did the same for me. She made promises to never fully leave and she never did. I could feel her in coincidences that I felt to be her—her love, her influence, her invisible guidance.

I never needed a study or scientists to tell me the remarkable capabilities of atoms and people but in case you do—you'll have it.

When you want to ignore life's potential, *read it.*
When you want to limit existence, *read it.*

When you want to reduce people to only physical presence when presence can be so very creative and inventive, *read it.*

Tuck it into your Bible to hold both faith and science simultaneously. They will both tell you the same thing: *I am always with you.*

My love hasn't gone anywhere.
It never will.

As for my influence and presence and existence—an atom, two places.
Two places at once, always.
Here and there.
With you and an immeasurable distance away in heaven.

Atoms—two places at once.
Me—two places at once.
One in spirit, one in entirety.
Both forever.

Never forget—I'm an atom.
We all are.

I love you always, from anywhere, from everywhere—two places at once.

love

This is for you. I've written the words over and over trying to get the message right, trying to find words you can return to again and again. Words you'll search for when my phone number has been given to someone else and my house has a new family inside.

Words for when I'm dead.

Why does that word sound so harsh? Maybe because it is. Maybe because we don't say it enough. Maybe because we wrap it like a present, hide it like a costume, in "gone" and "lost" and "passed."

They all mean the same. My time on earth has run out.

You probably wrote my obituary and most likely my eulogy too. I'm sure you listed all of my accomplishments from the world's view of success, from society's view of achievement. Did you forget my biggest, my best accomplishment, was always you?

Always you.

I'm writing it now so you can read it over and over, again and again, as many times as you need.

My biggest success, my biggest achievement, was always you.

You increased my capacity to love in ways I never knew possible. You did the same for my worry and my fear. I learned that's what love does. It repositions your priorities so that all you want is health and safety and happiness for those you love.

Every day I pray for your health, your safety, and your happiness. Every day I pray for you.

I bet even from heaven I'm praying for all of those same things. I imagine my prayers are protecting you from there now—still, always, protecting you. In fact, now they're closer to God. That must mean something, right?

I hope I not only told you but loved you so abundantly that my death could never erase that truth or its impact.

I love you—still, always, forever.

Hold that statement just as it is, never changing it to past tense. It is still love, even if it comes from heaven, even if it's given in new and creative ways.

Every time I rewrote this letter, I tried to include every sentiment, every thought, every single thing. But each time it had too much. Too many messages. Too many hopes.

Each time my only goal was a message that told you a million times, a billion times, that I love you.

I love you.
I love you.
I love you.

And every time it was in the present tense, just as it should be.
And I realized that is the message.
That is the hope—that you'll keep it that way—present.

Present

in your mind.
in your heart.
in your soul.
in your life.

I love you—present tense.
Now, always, forever.

because I love you

Because I love you, I don't tell you that you'll lose others. That more people in your life will die, either by age or disease or the unexpected.

I give you hugs and cuddles and truths that you can handle, truths that aren't heavier than your entire body, your entire being. I teach you all that I can, all that my heart is capable of.

I wonder, *Will I teach you grief, teach you mourning?*

The only morning you've ever known is the one announced by the sunrise and chanted by my one-of-a-kind wake-up song.

I cry and I hurt, but I do not tell you the truth of cemeteries and funerals, of eulogies and wills. I do not lie either. Instead, I wrap my words carefully in bandages of hope and faith and your youthful naivety.

Because I love you, I desperately try to protect you from the truth of life's fragility, of life's limitations and boundaries. Or maybe it's because I'm weak. Maybe both. Probably both—love and fear.

Last night I sat and made the plans for my mother's funeral and wrote her eulogy. Today we sit in those plans.

How does a mother learn grief and teach grief at the same time?

How does a mother lean into vulnerability and authenticity in ways that won't scare you or scar you?

I have no answers.

Only questions.

Only confusion and pain.

Only wonderings, only fears.
And love—yes, love too.

I say goodbye to my mother while you watch yours fall apart. I pray that my brokenness doesn't frighten you and also that it doesn't shatter you either. Even scarier, I pray that my jagged and splintered portions don't make you rough around the edges or hollow inside.

Because I love you, I want to shield you from all of this, but there isn't a shield that protects you from life, just like there isn't a shield to protect you from death. Those shields do not exist outside of fantasy and plotlines on screens.

For now, I will keep these harsh truths to myself. I will share only faith-filled hopes.

Because I love you, I won't teach you, yet, about grief and mourning. For now, I'll teach you about Jesus and heaven.

And hopefully, if I teach you well enough, the sting of those words, those truths, will be wrapped in the comfort and the truth of God.

Because I love you, I teach you to pray.

And then I pray.
And pray.
And pray.
And pray.

Because I love you.

unwritten

When I'm gone you might feel like someone has taken an eraser to each additional page of your story, to each upcoming chapter.

They haven't—not God or anyone.

You may feel otherwise, failing to realize your life's story has always been unwritten—each new day an opportunity to write what comes next. Each page written with what remains.

We who have died haven't been erased from your story, we've been repositioned—our presence exchanged for our influence. Both profound and meaningful.

Your life is unwritten in each new day because your life is real. It isn't a script. It isn't a novel. It's a work of truth, of heart, of meaning.

You are the only earthly author.

When grief enters your life you will feel a lack of control, a lack of authorship, a complete separation from the ability to create, to continue the story.

Remind yourself that I held my book. You hold your own.

Even with a story fully finished, my finest writing was the beginning of yours. Starting your story was my greatest masterpiece. *You are my greatest masterpiece.*

And now my story is complete. Its final words should read—*to be continued*, and in delicate fine print say, *in heaven*.

But yours, yours is filled with blank pages.

It's filled with opportunity.

It's filled with possibility
and hope
and promise.

Do not waste time searching for things that cannot be. Instead, carry forward with all that you can. I cannot be in your future in the ways we planned, in the ways we wanted, but I can still be a presence in your story.

You can, and will, be sad and hurting and confused and a thousand other things.

Do not be stuck.

Do not be paused.

Do not place a premature ending on pages with so much potential—your pages, your life.

Live and write. Write and live. Glance at the untouched and unwritten pages and dream. Get creative, both with my legacy and your own.

I imagine the libraries in heaven are filled with the fresh reflections of each day's words—each person's earthly authorship.

Write something I'd want to read, something I'd be proud of. *You're* something I'm proud of. Keep that going.

I look forward to watching you craft all that is currently unwritten.

when I go to heaven

If you knew how long I've waited to enter the infinity of heaven, if you knew how much this moment means to me, you'd be a little less sad, a little less sorrowful.

If you knew how happy I am, how renewed I've become, you'd be rejoicing along with me.

I never thought I'd love any place as much as the places with you, but this place, oh this place, it feels like home—like I'm where I belong.

It's a joy I can't describe.
It's a belonging that's too breathtaking for words.
It's a freedom with no limits, no expectations.

It's heaven.
I'm home in heaven.

If you could see from my perspective, if you could feel from my experience, you'd be thrilled for me. You'd have no fear of where I've ended up, you'd know it was perfection. I'm in the sacredness of perfection.

You'd still mourn.
You'd still cry and ache.
But you'd smile too.

You'd look up to the skies and know that I'm exactly where I always hoped I'd be—in forever.

If you could release yourself from the weight of grief and feel the liberation of my earthly suffering and struggle, you'd find your breath a little easier and your heartbeat would slow. You'd feel a calm, a comfort, in knowing my truth—my new beginning.

I would have stayed with you forever, if given the choice.
But I can't and I couldn't. That was never the plan, never the goal.

The vision, the hope, the dream, was always heaven.

Because heaven means together, not now, but one day.
Heaven means without end, eternally.

If you remind yourself that my lifelong mission was always to earn the infinity of heaven, you'll grieve a little easier and ache a little less. You'll count my newfound presence in everything you do instead of in the empty seat beside you. You'll count the laughs we shared and the hugs we exchanged more than the days I've been gone, the hours I won't get to experience.

If you knew how much I loved you when I was alive, you'll know how much I love you in death. It's the same, which means it still grows larger with each second, each minute. It always will.

If you only knew.
If you only knew.
If you only knew.

For now, you can't know, and that's a beautiful thing.

For now,
Know that I love you.
Know that I always will.
Know that I'm where I belong, where it feels like home.
Know I'm in heaven.

acknowledgments

My deepest appreciation goes to my mother and the advice she gave me when she was still here, alive. She encouraged me to write, and now that I finally have, it has changed my life in ways I could have never expected or planned for. I hope and pray that I am making her proud.

To my husband Justin—your mother created the greatest man I've ever known. She is undoubtedly proud of you, and the hope is that she'd be proud of *us*—a changed version of you, and me, a woman she never got to meet, though one I pray she can see from heaven. Her legacy is safe with you. *You are the love of my life. xox*

To my children, Hattie, Hutson & Hyland—you make me proud each and every day. I hope I make you proud too. I hope I live in a way that showcases my love for you. You are my heart. You are my everything. I hope one day, long from now, you'll remember me the way I remember my own mother, as someone whose love changes lives in beautiful and unforgettable ways. *xox*

To my sister—when I'm missing Mom with an intensity that won't dissipate, I look at you. You're so much like her. How lucky I am to have you as a sister, a friend, and a constant glimmer of Mom's greatness. *I love you. Be careful. You're pretty. xox*

To my dad—who's never read a full book, so he likely won't read this one, I love you. You may never read all my pages, but you've championed me in your own unforgettable way, writing letter after letter to the *Today Show* on my behalf. Your love shows up uniquely, and I am deeply grateful. *(PS—*Today Show, *he's still patiently waiting.)*

To Pops & Dede—the way you both live and love, the way you support and advocate, the way you remain unwavering with all of it, is one of the most inspiring things I've been able to witness. Thank you for being everything to everyone, all of the time.

To Rachel McRae and the entire team at Revell—you took a woman who sometimes didn't feel worthy enough for the pews of a church, let alone the shelves of a Christian publishing house, and you gave me a chance. Your belief in me changed my life. It restored my belief and my hope that even the broken, the imperfect, and the unknown are worthy of faith and also the hands and hearts of readers. Thank you.

To my agent, Debbie Alsdorf—you saw something in me, and in my pages, that I was still learning to see myself. Thank you for shepherding this work with such fierce faith and for walking beside me every step of the way.

To Lauren Flake, Natasha Smith, Sydnei Kaplan, Liz Newman, Brooke Tichenor, and all of the incredible writers and advocates in the grief community—thank you for being my safe space for the inner workings of this practice. You all get it in ways I wish you didn't have to, but you do. Thank you for your friendship and your encouragement. You keep me inspired and hopeful.

To Lisa Leshaw and my prayer team—you are proof that love, support, and guidance have no limits and no measurable boundaries. Without ever sharing the same room, the same space, you have protected and championed me in the beautiful ways my mother used to. And now, I swear she still is through all of you. *xox*

To the readers of *Happiness, Hope & Harsh Realities*—I hope *Legacy After Loss* met you where you are with truth, heart, and vulnerability. I hope it walked with you as you continue to step ahead, reminding you that you are never alone. As much as I want to make my mother proud, I want to make you proud too. I pray this book encouraged you in a real and lasting way. Thank you for reading my heart's work. My mother gave me the push and idea to write; you all gave me the opportunity. Without you, neither my first book, nor this one, would have been possible.

CHELSEA OHLEMILLER is a writer, speaker, and grief advocate who is best known for her authentic influence in living life with significant loss. After the untimely death of her mother, Chelsea created *Happiness, Hope & Harsh Realities*, a blog and social media brand that honors grief and creates a space for others to share in the vulnerable journey of one of life's most universal concepts. She's a sappy romantic, a die-hard Alabama fan and alum (Roll Tide!), a book collector, and a person who wears her heart on her sleeve. Her goal as a writer is to take real-life experiences, both the happy and the harsh, and turn them into something others can relate to. She lives in central Indiana with her husband and three children, who are all the driving force behind her passion to help and serve others.

Connect with Chelsea:

HopeAndHarshRealities.com

Facebook @HopeAndHarshRealities

Instagram @HopeAndHarshRealities

TikTok @ChelseaOhlemiller

hope FOR LIVING WITH *grief* FROM SOMEONE WHO *understands*

Grief changes everything. After the initial shock of losing someone you love fades, what comes next can feel uncertain—like you're standing in a life you no longer recognize, wondering how to move forward or if joy is still possible.

In this deeply personal and compassionate book, Chelsea Ohlemiller walks beside you through that uncertainty. Drawing from her own experience of loss, she offers a tender, honest exploration of what it means to live with grief. Through raw storytelling and thoughtful reflection, she gently guides you through the ache of absence while helping you rediscover meaning, connection, and even hope.

Rather than asking you to "move on," this book invites you to grow into something new—to navigate the emptiness without losing yourself, to carry love forward in new ways, and to find comfort in the memories that remain. It speaks to both the quiet strength it takes to honor a life while continuing to live your own and the enduring impact of the legacy your loved one leaves behind.

This honest yet hopeful book helps you learn what it looks like to live with grief—not by moving on but by remembering deeply, loving forward, and transforming memory into a lasting legacy.

CHELSEA OHLEMILLER is the author of *Now That She's Gone* and is well-known for her blog *Happiness, Hope & Harsh Realities*, where she examines the intersections of loss, healing, and the pursuit of meaning. Her essays have been featured in two Chicken Soup for the Soul collections and two Guideposts collections, as well as the national bestseller *So God Made a Mother*. She lives in Indianapolis with her husband and three children.

Revell
a division of Baker Publishing Group

US $19.99
Christian Living / Death, Grief, Bereavement
ISBN 978-0-8007-4815-9
51999
9 780800 748159
RevellBooks.com